500 FACTS
WARRIORS

500 FACTS
WARRIORS

First published in 2010 by Miles Kelly Publishing Ltd
Harding's Barn, Bardfield End Green, Thaxted, Essex, CM6 3PX, UK

2 4 6 8 10 9 7 5 3 1

Editorial Director Belinda Gallagher

Art Director Jo Brewer

Cover Designer Simon Lee

Designers Angela Ashton, Michelle Cannatella, Joe Jones,
Simon Lee, Andrea Slane

Junior Designer Kayleigh Allen

Editors Carly Blake, Rosie McGuire,
Sarah Parkin, Claire Philip

Indexer Indexing Specialists (UK) Ltd

Production Manager Elizabeth Collins

Reprographics Anthony Cambray, Stephan Davis,
Jennifer Hunt, Liberty Newton, Ian Paulyn

Assets Manager Bethan Ellish

Contributors John Farndon, Dr Gregory Fremont-Barnes,
Fiona Macdonald, John Malam, Rupert Matthews,
Philip Steele, Richard Tames, Jane Walker,

ISBN 978-1-84810-310-8

Printed in China

British Library Cataloguing-in-Publication Data
A catalogue record for this book is available from the British Library

Made with paper from a sustainable forest

www.mileskelly.net
info@mileskelly.net

www.factsforprojects.com

Self-publish your
children's book

buddingpress.co.uk

Contents

WHO DARES WINS

World of warriors

1 Warriors are people who fight in battles. A warrior is often a soldier or trained fighter who has shown great courage. Great warriors have the power to capture our imagination. Throughout history to the present day the cry of the warrior has been heard around the world.

▼ The ancient Greeks believed that a war was fought in the 1200s BC between the Greeks and the Trojans. In the story, Hector, a Trojan warrior, killed Patroclus, a Greek hero.

The first warriors

2 **The earliest warriors lived in prehistoric times.** Archaeologists divide prehistory into three ages. First the Stone Age, when stone was used to make tools and weapons. Then the Bronze Age, when metal was first used. After this came the Iron Age, when iron took over from bronze.

▲ The first axes were made from stone, such as flint. Flint axes were shaped from large blocks, and had very sharp cutting edges.

3 **Prehistoric people used a range of weapons.** Many axes, sling stones, arrows, swords and daggers survive today, but weapons made of perishable materials, such as wood, rotted away long ago. From the weapons that have survived, we can tell that prehistoric people lived in violent times.

4 **The first warriors must have been brave.** A fighter may have had to prove his bravery before becoming a warrior. He may have been set challenges to test his courage, or have been made to perform tasks in a ceremony. Only by passing the tests would he have been accepted as a warrior by the rest of his group.

◀ ▶ Weapons of prehistoric warriors – a spear, an axe and a sword.

Iron sword

Stone spear

Bronze axe

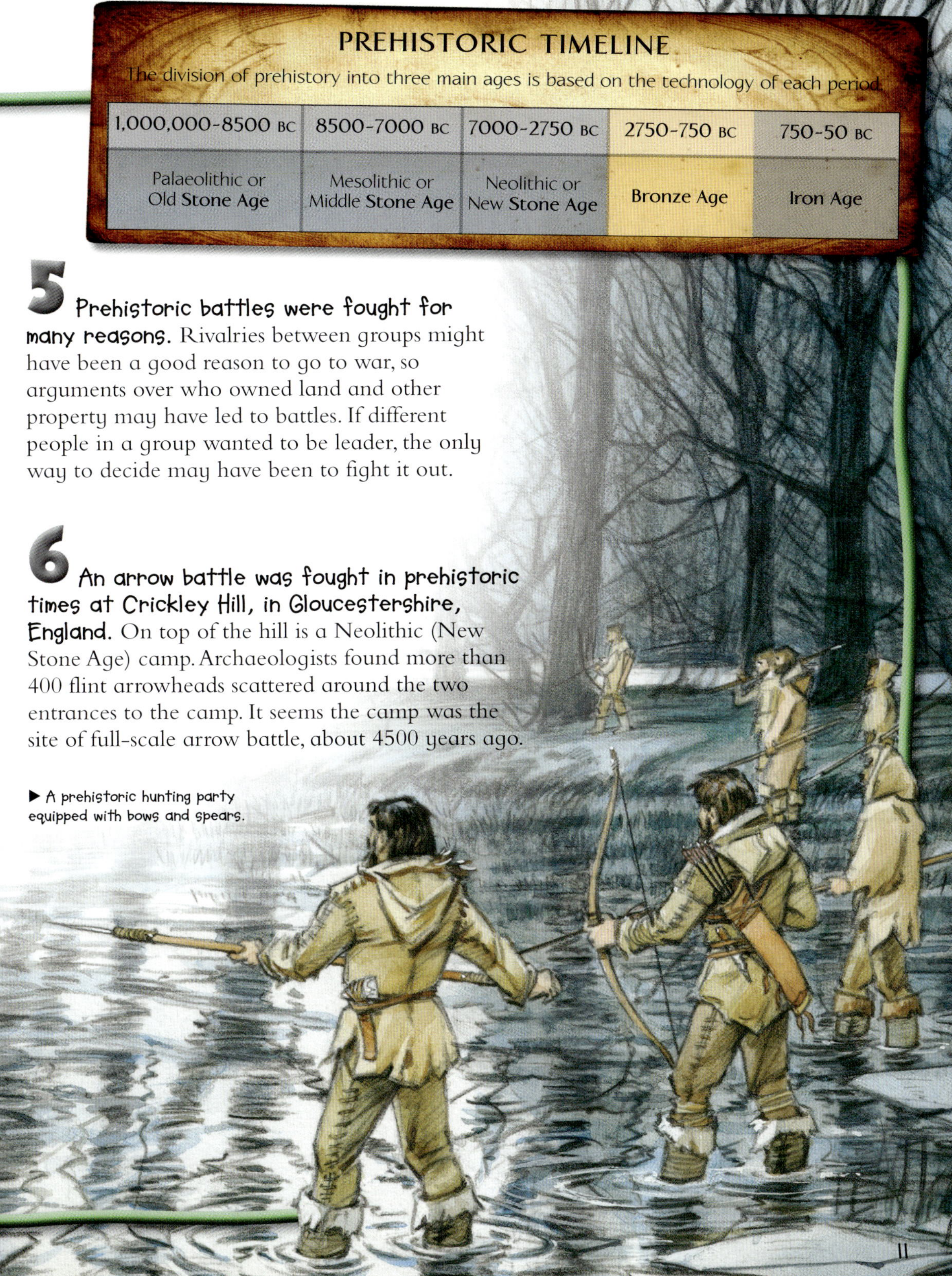

1,000,000-8500 BC	8500-7000 BC	7000-2750 BC	2750-750 BC	750-50 BC
Palaeolithic or Old Stone Age	Mesolithic or Middle Stone Age	Neolithic or New Stone Age	Bronze Age	Iron Age

5 **Prehistoric battles were fought for many reasons.** Rivalries between groups might have been a good reason to go to war, so arguments over who owned land and other property may have led to battles. If different people in a group wanted to be leader, the only way to decide may have been to fight it out.

6 **An arrow battle was fought in prehistoric times at Crickley Hill, in Gloucestershire, England.** On top of the hill is a Neolithic (New Stone Age) camp. Archaeologists found more than 400 flint arrowheads scattered around the two entrances to the camp. It seems the camp was the site of full-scale arrow battle, about 4500 years ago.

▶ A prehistoric hunting party equipped with bows and spears.

Warriors of Mesopotamia

7 **The first armies were in Mesopotamia – a region of the Middle East where present-day Iran and Iraq are found.** Here, men were first organized into fighting forces around 4500 years ago. Kings wanted to show power, and controlling an army was a way to do this. King Sargon (2334–2279 BC) was the first Mesopotamian ruler to have a full-time army.

▲ Mesopotamia was an area of the Middle East between the rivers Euphrates and Tigris.

I DON'T BELIEVE IT!

Using a composite bow, a Mesopotamian archer could fire an arrow up to about 245 metres.

8 **Mesopotamian armies had hundreds of thousands of troops.** They were organized into foot soldiers (infantry), horse soldiers (cavalry) and the most feared of all – charioteers. Chariots were wheeled, horse-drawn platforms for archers to shoot arrows from. Some battles involved hundreds of chariots.

▲ Mounted archers were a rapid strike force of Assyrian armies. Assyria was a kingdom of northern Mesopotamia.

10 **The Battle of Carchemish was fought in 605 BC.** It was between the Babylonians (one of the peoples of Mesopotamia) and the ancient Egyptians. The Babylonian army destroyed the Egyptian army, and the surviving Egyptian forces fled. The Babylonians gave chase, and a second battle took place near the Sea of Galilee, in Palestine. The Egyptians were defeated again, and retreated into Egypt.

11 **Mesopotamian myths tell of warrior heroes.** The greatest was Gilgamesh who, according to legend, defeated evil monsters. On a quest for immortality (eternal life), Gilgamesh was set a test to stay awake for seven nights. But he fell asleep, failing the test, and so never became immortal.

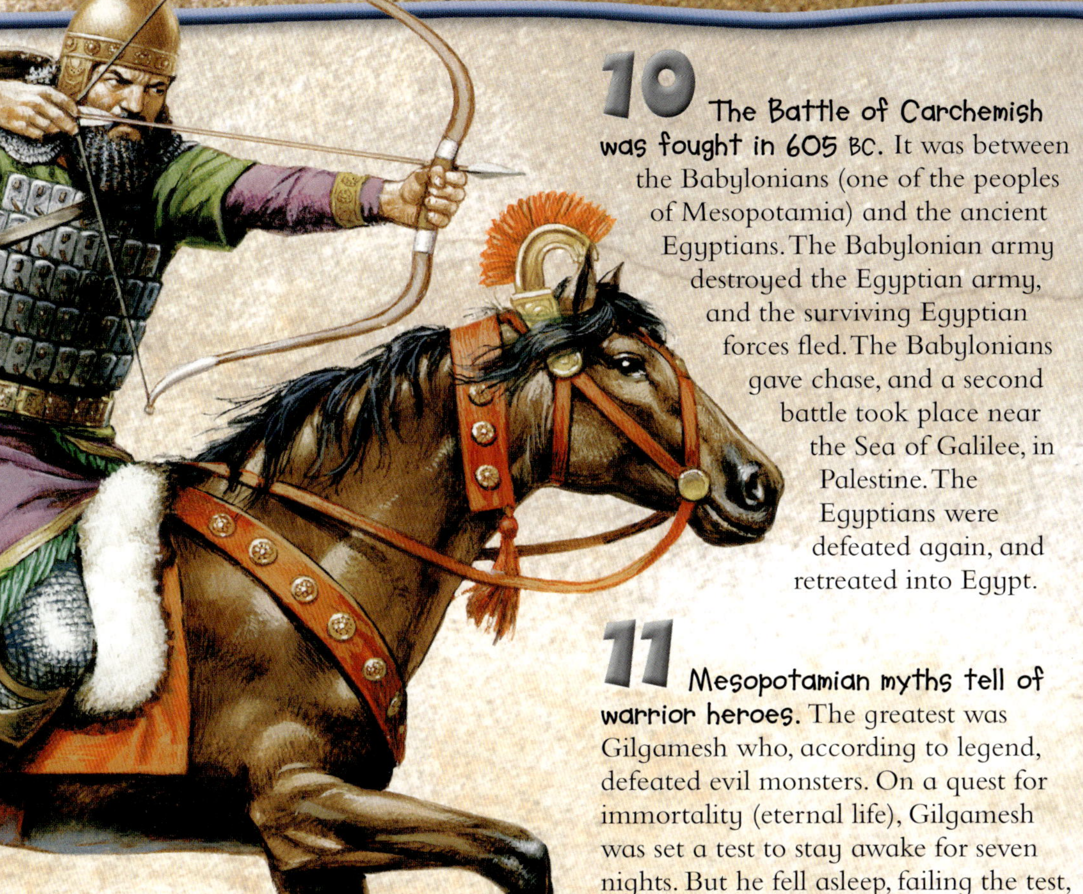

▶ In the legend of Gilgamesh, the warrior Gilgamesh killed a hideous giant called Humbaba.

9 **The Mesopotamian warrior's main weapon was the bow.** At first, bows were made from single pieces of wood, but then people discovered how to make bows from layers of wood and bone glued together. These were called composite bows, and they fired arrows further than one-piece bows.

Ramesses II

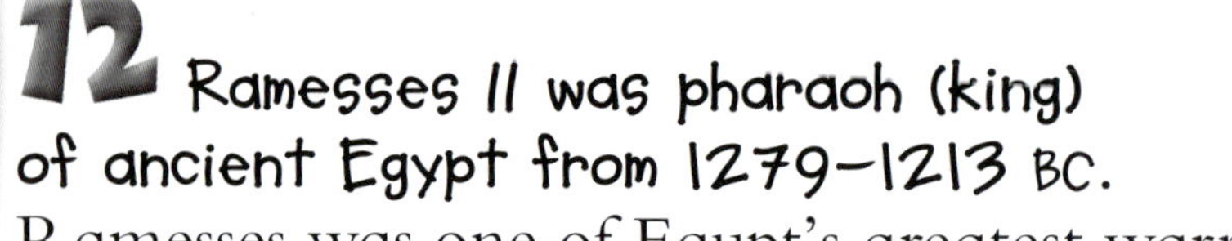

12 Ramesses II was pharaoh (king) of ancient Egypt from 1279–1213 BC. Ramesses was one of Egypt's greatest warrior pharaohs, and because he conquered Egypt's enemies he became known as Ramesses the Great. He is best known for leading his forces against the Hittites in the Battle of Kadesh.

13 The army of Ramesses II had about 20,000 warriors. Armies were organized into divisions of about 5000 men, who were mostly infantry soldiers. There were also charioteers, who steered chariots as their passengers shot arrows or threw spears. Chariots caused panic, smashing through enemy front lines at up to 38 kilometres an hour.

◄ Stone statues of Ramesses II were put up all over ancient Egypt.

QUIZ

1. In what year did Ramesses II become pharaoh?
2. What was the top speed of an Egyptian chariot?
3. Where did the Hittites come from?
4. When was the Battle of Kadesh?
5. What was the outcome of the Battle of Kadesh?

Answers:
1. 1279 BC
2. About 38 kilometres an hour
3. Turkey 4. 1275 BC 5. A draw

◄ Egyptian charioteers were skilled warriors and struck fear into the enemy.

14 **Egyptian infantry soldiers fought with spears, axes, curved swords and daggers.** Archers used powerful bows that shot arrows tipped with points of chipped stone. Instead of wearing armour, warriors protected themselves with leather or wooden shields.

15 **Before Ramesses II, Tuthmosis III waged war against Egypt's neighbours to the north-east.** Tuthmosis was very successful, but the Hittites (a warlike people from an area that is now Turkey) also wanted to control this region, and they became Egypt's bitter enemies.

16 **Ramesses II fought the Hittites in 1275 BC at Kadesh (in modern-day Syria) because the Hittites were threatening to invade Egypt.** It was probably the largest chariot battle ever fought, involving 5000–6000 chariots. At first, the Hittites were winning, and the Egyptians retreated. Then Ramesses stopped the panic among his troops and fought back. The Hittites retreated into the city of Kadesh. Both sides claimed they had won.

► The Egyptian Empire stretched to the borders of present-day Turkey.

Warriors of ancient Greece

17 Foot soldiers called hoplites formed the core of every ancient Greek army. Each of the city-states of Greece had its own army of fighting men. Rival cities went to war on many occasions, but they also came together to fight a common enemy, usually the Persians.

▲ Ancient Greece was divided into city-states. Each one was a city and the surrounding territory.

▶ A hoplite was named after his *hoplon* (shield).

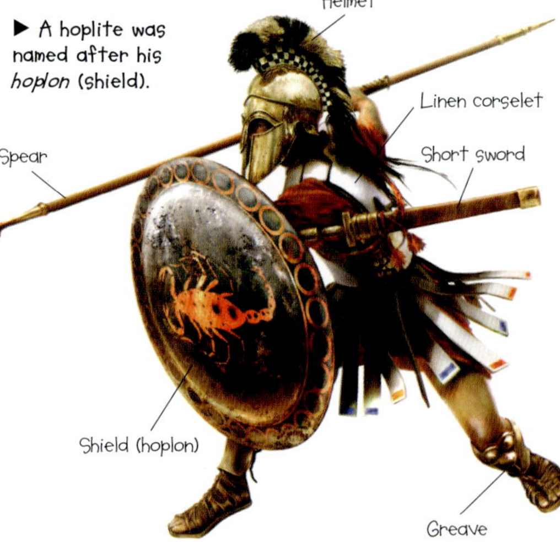

18 A hoplite carried a large round shield, a long spear and a short sword. His body armour was a bronze helmet, a stiff linen corselet (tunic), and bronze greaves (leg guards). This was the standard equipment for all hoplites, regardless of their city-state.

19 Battles took place on flat, open plains. Hoplite ranks stood in a formation called a phalanx. It was six to eight ranks deep, with hundreds of men in each rank. The phalanxes marched towards each other, with the first three ranks holding their spears level, pointing at the enemy.

◀ When armies met, the front soldiers thrust their spears into each other's phalanx, while the men at the back pushed their comrades forward.

20 In the city-state of Sparta all men were raised to be warriors. Training began in childhood. Children went about barefoot and were lightly dressed, even in winter. This was supposed to toughen them up. At 20 they were sent away to join other soldiers. The key to Spartan success on the battlefield was discipline.

▶ The warrior Achilles, as seen in the film *Troy* (Warner Brothers, 2004). He was one of the greatest heroes of ancient Greece.

21 Achilles was a mythological Greek warrior. As a baby, his mother took him by the heel and dipped him in the River Styx. The only part of him untouched by the water was his heel. The river's magical waters gave him great strength but his undipped heel was his weak spot. Achilles fought in the war against the Trojans. He defeated Hector, their champion fighter, and seemed unstoppable. He was only killed when an arrow struck him in the heel.

Alexander

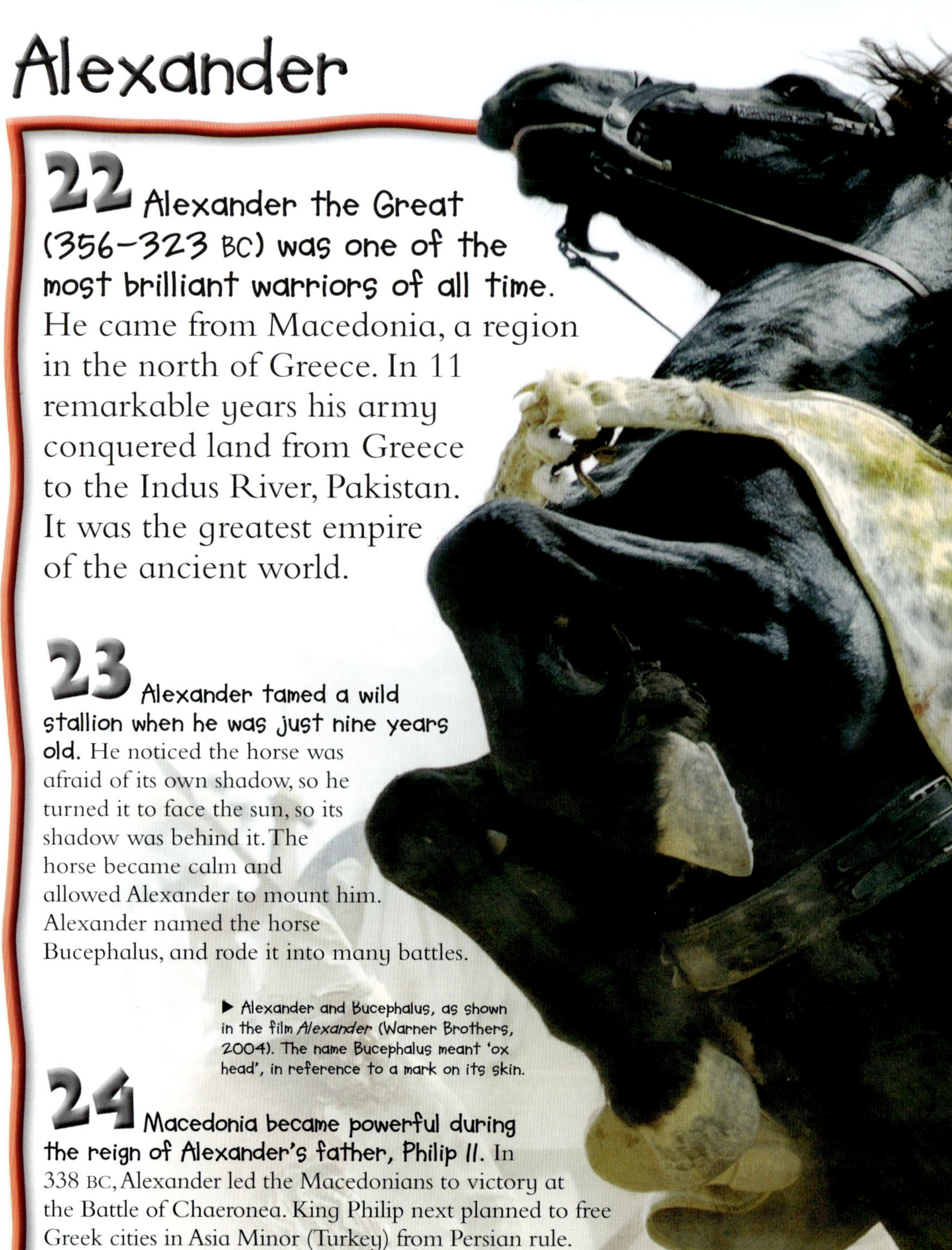

22 Alexander the Great (356–323 BC) was one of the most brilliant warriors of all time. He came from Macedonia, a region in the north of Greece. In 11 remarkable years his army conquered land from Greece to the Indus River, Pakistan. It was the greatest empire of the ancient world.

23 Alexander tamed a wild stallion when he was just nine years old. He noticed the horse was afraid of its own shadow, so he turned it to face the sun, so its shadow was behind it. The horse became calm and allowed Alexander to mount him. Alexander named the horse Bucephalus, and rode it into many battles.

▶ Alexander and Bucephalus, as shown in the film *Alexander* (Warner Brothers, 2004). The name Bucephalus meant 'ox head', in reference to a mark on its skin.

24 Macedonia became powerful during the reign of Alexander's father, Philip II. In 338 BC, Alexander led the Macedonians to victory at the Battle of Chaeronea. King Philip next planned to free Greek cities in Asia Minor (Turkey) from Persian rule. When his father died, Alexander decided to carry out his plans.

25 Alexander raised an army of 43,000 hoplites and 5500 cavalry. Soon after entering the Persian Empire, Alexander's army defeated a Persian army at the Battle of the Granicus River (334 BC). This opened the way to the Greek cities of Asia Minor, which Alexander freed from Persian control.

▶ The Battle of the Granicus River was fought in present-day Turkey.

26 Alexander's greatest battle against the Persians was the Battle of Issus in 333 BC. His army of 35,000 troops met the army of Darius III, king of Persia, at Issus, in modern-day southern Turkey. Alexander's army was victorious, despite being outnumbered two to one. Later that year he defeated them at the Battle of Gaugamela (in present-day Iraq). Then Alexander led his army into the heart of the Persian Empire, taking city after city.

▶ A mosaic of the Battle of Issus, showing Darius III and his army.

Julius Caesar

27 **Julius Caesar (100–44 BC) was the greatest Roman general.** He was highly successful, defeating the Gauls (tribes that lived in present-day France and Belgium) and invading Britain in 55 BC and 54 BC. Caesar then led his troops into Italy and fought a civil war to rule the Roman world. He won, and was made 'dictator for life', but was stabbed to death in 44 BC.

28 **As a young man, Caesar was captured by pirates.** He was caught when sailing to the Mediterranean island of Rhodes. The pirates held him until a ransom was paid. Caesar vowed to hunt the pirates down. All of them were found and executed on his orders.

29 **Caesar led the best army of the time.** Roman soldiers (legionaries) were armed with a dagger, a short sword and a javelin. They wore helmets and armour made from metal and leather and carried shields. For long-distance fighting, a *ballista* fired big arrows with iron tips. In siege warfare an *onager* hurled rocks onto enemy defences.

I DON'T BELIEVE IT!

A skeleton from Maiden Castle in Dorset, England, had a ballista bolt in its spine – evidence of a battle between Britons and Romans.

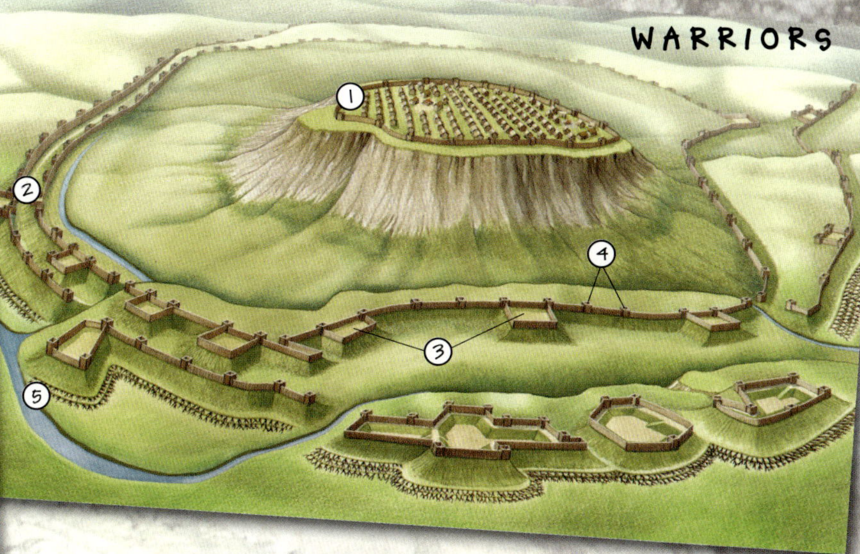

▶ Caesar's plan at Alesia was to starve the Gauls into surrender. It worked.

Key

1. Hilltop fort of Alesia
2. First ditch and wall traps Gauls
3. Roman camps
4. Roman look-out points
5. Second ditch and wall keeps Romans safe

▼ Roman legionaries (soldiers) preparing a ballista to fire a bolt.

30 **Caesar led his army into Gaul, planning to make it part of the Roman world.** For seven years, battles were fought between the Romans and the tribes of Gaul. When a group of tribes (led by the Gallic chief Vercingetorix) rebelled, Caesar took action to end the revolt.

31 **Vercingetorix led an army of Gauls against the Romans in 52 BC.** The Romans forced the Gauls back to their hilltop fortress at Alesia, France. Caesar's troops encircled the hill with huge ditches. One kept the Gauls trapped inside, and the other protected the Romans from the Gauls' allies. Realizing that he could not win, Vercingetorix surrendered.

Boudicca

32 **Boudicca was a warrior queen.** She was from a Celtic tribe called the Iceni, which lived in the east of Britain. A Roman writer described Boudicca as tall, with long red hair, and wearing a large gold necklace. Boudicca is famous for leading an uprising against the Romans.

33 **Boudicca's husband, King Prasutagus, died around AD 60.** He left half his kingdom to the Romans and the other half to Boudicca. The Romans wanted all of it, and set about taking it by force. So during AD 60 and AD 61, Boudicca led the Iceni and other British tribes in a rebellion against the Romans.

▶ Boudicca, warrior queen of the Iceni, fought the Romans in Britain.

34 **Boudicca is said to have led more than 100,000 warriors against the Romans.** Known as the Britons, they fought with swords and spears, and protected themselves with shields. Some rode into battle in chariots. They were brave warriors, but were not as organized as the Romans.

35 Boudicca's warriors went south, to the Roman towns of south-east Britain. They burned the towns of Camulodunum (Colchester), Londinium (London) and Verulamium (St Albans), killing some 70,000 civilians and destroying the Roman IXth Legion.

36 Boudicca's last battle was somewhere in the English Midlands. As many as 230,000 Britons fought a smaller Roman force. The Romans had better tactics and weapons, and 80,000 Britons are said to have died. The Romans won, and Boudicca died soon after the battle, possibly ending her own life with poison.

Ivar the Boneless

 Ivar Ragnarsson was a Viking warrior from Scandinavia, in northern Europe. His nickname was 'Ivar the Boneless', which may have been linked to a Viking story about a man whose bones shrivelled because he had done something really bad. Ivar was a leader of the Great Army, a force of Vikings that invaded England in AD 865.

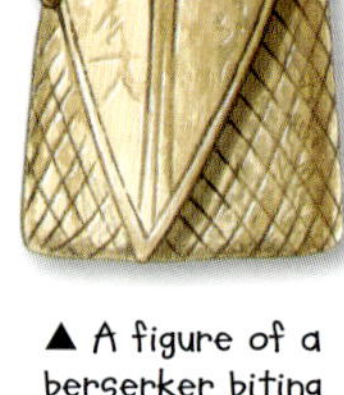

▲ A figure of a berserker biting his shield.

 Ivar the Boneless was a berserker – the bravest of all Viking warriors. Berserkers worked themselves up in preparation for battle by shouting and biting the edges of their shields. They wore no armour and felt they had the strength of wild beasts. The word 'beserker' is the origin of the expression 'to go berserk'.

 Viking warbands struck fear into the people of western and northern Europe. In November AD 866, the Viking Great Army captured the Anglo-Saxon town of York in northern England. Ivar was probably one of the warriors who helped take the town. York became the capital of the Viking kingdom in England.

▼ Viking warriors travelled in longships. These could be rowed inland along rivers.

▶ Ragnar Lodbrok is said to have fought incredible creatures.

40 According to Viking stories, Ivar's father was Ragnar Lodbrok. His name means 'hairy trousers'. Ragnar may be a legendary Viking, only existing in mythology. He was said to have fought battles across the Viking world and killed giant serpents. He earned his nickname because he wore shaggy trousers.

▶ Many Viking weapons and pieces of armour have been found.

Iron helmet

Spear

Knife

41 The main Viking weapon was the iron sword. Other weapons included spears tipped with iron, battleaxes and bows and arrows. A few warriors wore chainmail armour, while others wore leather waistcoats. Some wore iron helmets, but most made do with leather caps. They carried round shields made from wood and leather.

Norman warriors

42 In AD 911, a Viking warband led by Rollo arrived in northern France. At first the region was known as *Nordmannia* ('Northman's Land'). The Vikings settled in the area and it became known as Normandy. The warriors who came from this area were the Normans.

▲ In 1066, the Normans departed from St Valery in northern France and landed at Pevensey in southern England, ready to do battle.

43 The Normans were skilled fighters, organizers and builders. In the AD 1000s Norman armies conquered England, much of France, southern Italy and Sicily. They took part in the Crusades to the Holy Land (Palestine), and built many strong buildings.

44 A Norman army was made up of many foot soldiers. They fought with spears, axes, and bows. The cavalry was the strongest part of the army. Cavalry soldiers owned their own horses and went to war in the hope of being rewarded for their service.

45 In battle, Norman foot soldiers formed themselves into defensive shield walls or war hedges. The front ranks held their long shields close together, forming a solid barrier that protected the warriors behind it from missiles. The shield wall came apart to allow the fighters to use their weapons, and for the cavalry to charge through.

46 On 28 September 1066, William, Duke of Normandy invaded England. He led about 750 ships across the English Channel from France. On board was an army of 10,000 men and 3000 horses. On 14 October 1066, the Normans defeated the English in the Battle of Hastings. Harold, the king of England, was killed, and William became England's first Norman king. He was known as William the Conqueror.

◀ At Senlac Hill, near Hastings, Norman soldiers charged uphill to attack the English.

QUIZ

1. What area of France did the Normans come from?
2. What was the strongest part of a Norman army?
3. In what year was the Battle of Hastings?

Answers:
1. Normandy
2. The cavalry 3. 1066

Saladin

47 Saladin (1137–1193) was a Muslim warrior. He led a religious war (*jihad*) in the Middle East. Saladin (or Salah ad-Din Yuseuf) became a soldier at 14, and for many years fought against other Muslims in Egypt. By 1187, he had become the sultan (ruler) of Egypt and Syria, and decided to drive Christians out of the holy city of Jerusalem.

▲ Both sides used mounted troops in their battles.

▲ Routes taken by Crusader armies as they travelled to the Holy Land.

48 **The Battle of Hattin was fought in July 1187.** It was a major battle between Muslims, led by Saladin, and Christians, led by Guy of Lusignan, and took place near Lake Tiberias in northern Palestine. Guy had about 20,000 troops, but Saladin's army was half as big again. Perhaps as few as 3000 Christian warriors survived the battle. It was an important victory for Saladin.

◄ Muslim warriors were lightly armoured and fought with curved swords.

49 **The series of religious wars fought in the Holy Land (Palestine) between Muslims and Christians were called Crusades.** Between 1096 and 1291, Christian soldiers travelled from Europe to the Holy Land, where they fought to curb the spread of Islam, save Jerusalem, and protect Christian pilgrims who went there.

50 **After the Battle of Hattin, Saladin conquered Christian strongholds in the Holy Land.** He took Acre and Jaffa in present-day Israel, and Beirut in Lebanon. By September 1187 his army reached Jerusalem. The Christians surrendered after a short siege. Saladin showed some mercy, allowing some Christians to leave the city in return for a ransom. The rest he sold into slavery.

51 **Saladin's warriors were mostly lightly armed mounted archers.** They wore little body armour, so they could ride much faster than their Christian foes who wore heavy metal armour. Speed was the Muslim warriors' secret of success. They preferred to engage in skirmishes, picking off their enemies with well-aimed arrows before making their escape. This way, they weakened their opponents.

▶ The forces of Saladin's army besiege the city of Jerusalem in 1187, as shown in the film *Kingdom of Heaven* (Twentieth Century Fox, 2005).

Richard the Lionheart

52 King Richard I (1157–1199) was king of England for ten years, from 1189 to 1199. He was known as *Coeur de Lion*, or Richard the Lionheart, because of his success as a military leader and warrior.

▶ King Richard I led an army of crusaders to the Holy Land.

53 Richard, the Holy Roman Emperor Frederick I (king of Germany and Italy), and King Philip II of France organized a crusade to free Jerusalem from Saladin. This was the Third Crusade, and lasted from 1189 to 1192. On reaching the Holy Land, the first action of Richard's knights was to capture the city of Acre from the Muslims. He did this in July 1191, with the use of battering rams and catapults.

54 After taking Acre, Richard marched towards Jerusalem. His progress was stopped in September 1191, when he fought Saladin at the Battle of Arsuf. The Christian and Muslim armies each had about 20,000 warriors, and although the battle was a victory for Richard, Saladin's army was able to regroup and continue with its hit-and-run skirmishes.

55 **Richard came to within about 19 kilometres of Jerusalem.** He was unable to attack it as his supplies were low and Saladin's constant skirmishes had picked off too many of his troops. The two leaders made peace, and in return for Richard agreeing to leave, Saladin allowed Christian pilgrims to visit Jerusalem, ending the Third Crusade.

56 **The crusaders set sail for home, but Richard's adventures weren't over.** While travelling overland from Venice, he was captured by an Austrian enemy, and handed over to Henry VI of Germany. A ransom of 150,000 silver marks (a unit of currency) was demanded for his release. After being held for over a year, the ransom was paid, and Richard returned home.

Warrior monks

57 Crusader armies were composed of foot soldiers and mounted knights. Among the knights were warriors who belonged to religious groups or orders. They followed strict rules, and were organized in a similar way to monks in monasteries. These 'warrior monks' were anything but peaceful.

Medieval knights carried shields made of wood and covered with coloured leather. They had pictures or patterns (coats of arms) on them so knights could recognize their friends in battle. Look for pictures of shields in books or on the Internet. Then have a go at drawing and colouring a design of your own.

58 The Knights Hospitaller were founded in Jerusalem in 1099. At first their role was to provide safe lodgings for Christian pilgrims to the city, and to care for the sick and wounded in their hospital. This gradually became a sizeable military force, acting as armed guards for pilgrims and crusaders. The Knights Hospitaller were also known as the Knights of St John.

▶ The symbol of the Knights Templar – two knights on one horse.

59 The Knights Templar were founded in Jerusalem in 1119 by nine French knights. They were called Templars because their headquarters was a building on the site of the Temple of Solomon. Knights Templar were the best disciplined and bravest crusaders. They were also the richest, thanks to donations from Christians in Europe.

60 The German Teutonic Knights were founded at Acre in 1198. They were formed to protect Christian pilgrims, but took up arms against Muslims and built castles. Active in the Holy Land until the 1290s, their main work was carried out later in the Baltic region, fighting in Lithuania.

◀ Knights took part in jousting tournaments, charging at each other with lances.

61 The armoured knight was the elite warrior of medieval Europe. In childhood he was taught to ride and to use a sword and lance. As a knight, he took part in tournaments to improve his fighting skills, ready for when he went to war.

▶ Knights marched with colourful pennants (triangular flags).

Genghis Khan

62 **Mongol warrior Genghis Khan (1162–1227) ruled with great discipline.** He was born in Mongolia, and given the name Temujin. The Mongols were one of many tribes that lived on the grassy plains (steppe) of central Asia. They were horsemen who followed their herds of grazing animals.

▲ Genghis Khan was a fearless warrior who led his Mongol troops to victory.

63

The Mongol tribes were constantly at war with each other. Temujin set about uniting the tribes, and in 1206 he became ruler (*khan*) of them all. From then on he was known as Genghis Khan, meaning 'Ruler of the Earth'. His armies conquered almost all of China. By the time he died, his empire stretched from the Black Sea to the Pacific Ocean – it was the largest empire in history.

64

Mongol warriors wore leather armour and helmets and fired arrows from powerful bows as they rode. Soldiers also carried swords, maces, axes and sometimes short spears with hooks on their points. Mongol warriors each had a string of horses, and changed their mounts often, so as not to tire them.

▶ The Mongol Empire covered much of Asia and beyond.

65

Mongol warriors were organized into large groups, which were divided into units of ten (an *arban*). In battle, they would pretend to flee to make their enemy give chase. When the pursuing troops became disorganized the Mongols would turn on them, closing in to trap them.

66

The Battle of the Indus River was fought in 1221, in present–day Pakistan. A Mongol army of 10,000 faced Muslim troops of 5000 on the banks of the river. The Mongols inflicted heavy losses, and only a few Muslim soldiers crossed the river to safety.

◀ Mongol cavalrymen were expert archers. Some arrows they used made whistling noises and were used to send signals.

Joan of Arc

▲ France, showing the area controlled by the English.

67 Born in France, Joan of Arc (1412–1431) lived at a time when large parts of France were controlled by the English. When Joan was about 12, she believed she had a vision in which the patron saints of France commanded her to dress as a man and lead the fight to rid France of the English.

▼ Joan of Arc was easy to spot on the battlefield because she wore a suit of white armour.

68 Joan lived during the Hundred Years' War. This was a series of wars between England and France that began in 1337. The wars were fought over English claims to be the rulers of France. Joan went to see France's *Dauphin* (crown prince), who was soon to become King Charles VII, and told him of her vision.

69 Charles gave Joan permission to travel to the city of Orléans with a French army. The city was under siege from the English. The army arrived in April 1429. Joan was dressed as a knight, and carried a banner. Within a week, the English retreated. From then on, Joan was known as the 'Maid of Orléans'.

70 **For the next 12 months, Joan led the French in battles against the English.** She won back territory for France. In May 1430, Joan was captured by the Duke of Burgundy (a French nobleman on the side of the English). She became a prisoner-of-war, and was eventually sold to the English.

▶ Saint Joan of Arc is one of the most popular saints of the Roman Catholic Church.

71 **The English put Joan on trial.** She was tried as a witch and a heretic (a person who goes against the teachings of the Christian church), found guilty, and sentenced to death. In May 1431, Joan was burnt at the stake in the French city of Rouen. She was declared innocent 25 years after her death, and in 1920 the Pope made her a saint.

Moctezuma

72 The Aztecs lived in the present-day country of Mexico. They were fierce warriors who defeated rival tribes to become the strongest group in the region. The last Aztec emperor was called Moctezuma II (*c.*1480–1520). He became leader of the Aztecs in 1502. He was a powerful and ruthless leader who was feared and admired by his people.

▲ Moctezuma was regarded as a god by the Aztec people.

73 The Aztecs were a warlike people. Every able-bodied man was expected to fight in Moctezuma's army. They were taught to use weapons as children, and at 15 they were old enough to go to war. It was considered an honour to fight for the emperor. Warriors who did well were rewarded with gifts of land and slaves.

74

The fiercest Aztec fighters were the Eagle and Jaguar warriors. Eagle warriors wore suits made from feathers and Jaguar warriors dressed in ocelot skins. They were full-time soldiers, while the bulk of the army were part-time soldiers who returned to regular jobs after the fighting was over.

75

Fighters fought with slings, bows and spears launched from spear-throwers. The most dangerous Aztec weapon was the war-club, the edges of which were covered with blades of razor-sharp obsidian (a glass-like stone made inside volcanoes). It could slice an enemy's head off in one blow.

▶ A warrior's most important job was to capture prisoners for sacrifice. The more prisoners he took, the more important he became.

▼ The Aztecs outnumbered the Spaniards, but the Spaniards had better weapons.

76

In 1519, an army of Spaniards landed in Mexico in search of gold. When the news reached Moctezuma, he thought they were gods and sent them gifts, and when they first arrived in the Aztec capital he treated them as guests. He soon realized his mistake. Fighting between the Aztecs and the Spaniards began in May 1520. Moctezuma was killed, and the Aztec city was looted and destroyed.

Key

1. Eagle warrior in a suit of feathers
2. Fur and feather shield
3. Wooden club with shards of obsidian
4. Jaguar warrior
5. Spear tipped with obsidian

Babur

77 The founder of the Mughal Empire in northern India is known as Babur (1483–1531). His real name was Zahir ud-Din Muhammad, but as he rose to power he was given the nickname Babur, meaning 'tiger'. He was a powerful Muslim leader.

▲ The Battle of Khanwa (1527) gave Babur control of northern India.

◄ The extent of the Mughal empire in India.

80 In the Battle of Panipat, Babur's warriors used gunpowder weapons called arquebuses. They were an early type of bullet-firing gun, and were the most up-to-date weapons of the time. The traditional weapons of Mughal warriors were a sword with a curved blade (*talwar*) and a mace. They wore chainmail armour and carried a small round shield (*dahl*).

78 In 1504, Babur and a group of Muslim fighters captured Kabul, in Afghanistan. He established a small kingdom there, and began making raids into northern India. In 1525, he was asked to attack Ibrahim Lodi, the sultan (ruler) of Delhi, so Babur mounted a full-scale invasion of northern India.

79 Babur and Lodi's armies met at Panipat, India, in 1526. Babur had 25,000 troops, Lodi had 40,000. Lodi struck first, but failed to break through Babur's line of 700 carts tied together. After defeating Lodi's army, Babur marched to Delhi, which became the capital of the Mughal empire.

▼► Weapons of Babur's Mughal warriors.

Mace

Knife

81 **The largest part of Babur's army was the cavalry.** He could muster tens of thousands of horsemen, who served as archers, and were his elite troops. His foot soldiers were peasants who were forced to fight. Mughal armies also made use of war elephants, which acted as firing platforms for archers and spear-throwers. Because of their height, elephants were also used as command and observation posts.

▶ War elephants were used by Mughal and other armies in India. Some elephants wore armour.

Napoleon Bonaparte

82 French general Napoleon Bonaparte (1769–1821) trained as a soldier from the age of ten. At 27 he was in charge of the French army in Italy. For a short time, he ruled a large part of Europe, creating the largest empire in Europe since the time of the Romans.

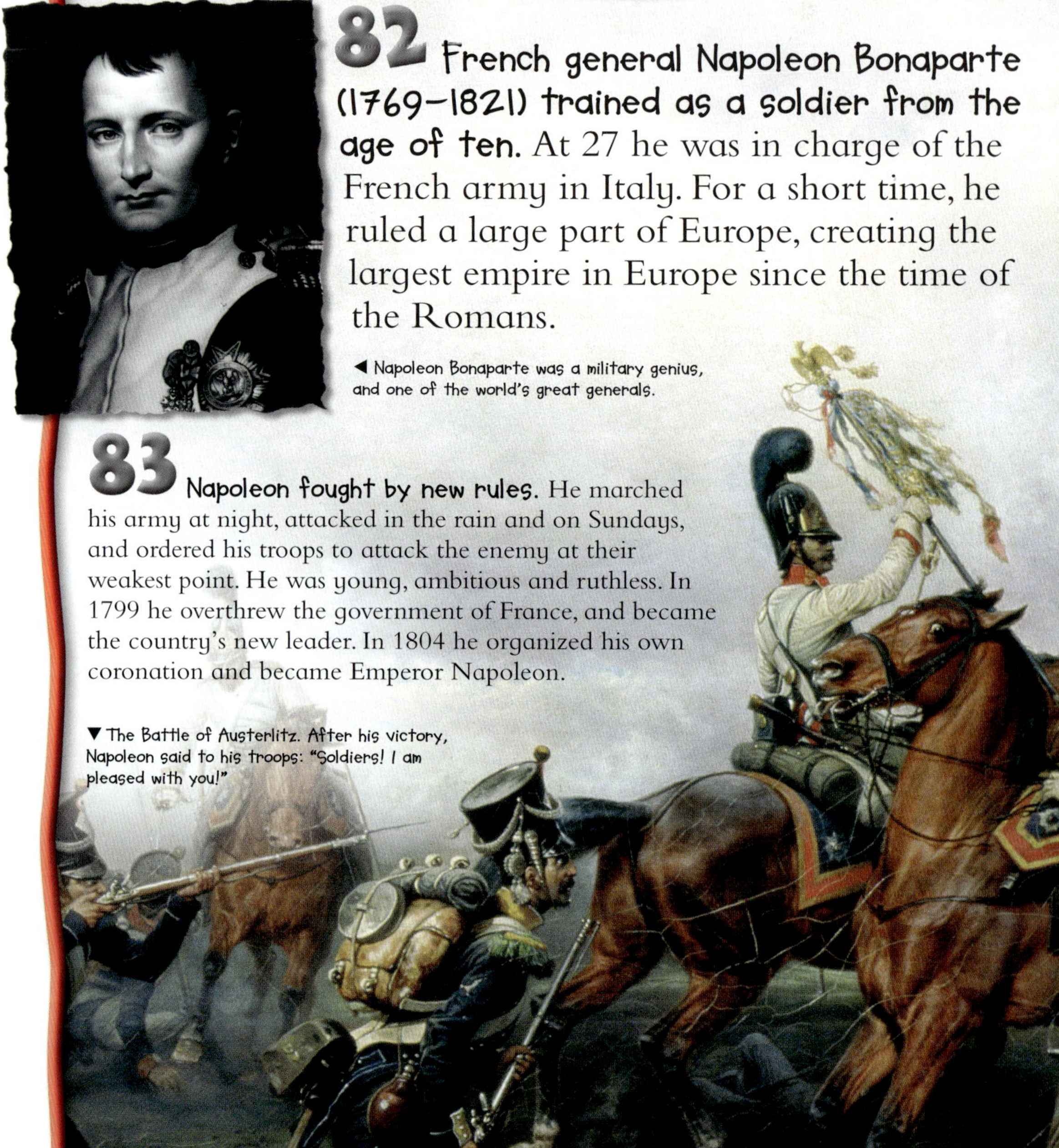

◀ Napoleon Bonaparte was a military genius, and one of the world's great generals.

83 Napoleon fought by new rules. He marched his army at night, attacked in the rain and on Sundays, and ordered his troops to attack the enemy at their weakest point. He was young, ambitious and ruthless. In 1799 he overthrew the government of France, and became the country's new leader. In 1804 he organized his own coronation and became Emperor Napoleon.

▼ The Battle of Austerlitz. After his victory, Napoleon said to his troops: "Soldiers! I am pleased with you!"

▶ The extent of Napoleon's French Empire across Europe.

84 **Napoleon's greatest victory was the Battle of Austerlitz.** It was fought on 2 December, 1805, in the present-day Czech Republic. Napoleon had 70,000 troops. They faced a combined army of 80,000 Russians and Austrians. The victory was a turning point for Napoleon, who sensed he could be master of all Europe.

85 **In 1812, Napoleon set his sights on Russia.** He invaded with an army of half-a-million men, and the Russians retreated. He reached Moscow, but the Russians refused to make peace. Far from home, and with supplies running low, Napoleon had no choice but to retreat. It was a bitterly cold winter, and thousands of soldiers froze to death on the march home.

86 **In 1814, Austria, Russia, Prussia and Britain attacked France.** They reached Paris, and Napoleon was banished to the island of Elba in the Mediterranean. He escaped and returned to France to gather a new army. His last battle was at Waterloo, on 18 June, 1815. He was defeated by an army of British and Prussians and sent to the island of St Helena in the Atlantic Ocean, where he died six years later.

I DON'T BELIEVE IT!

Napoleon was supposed to be crowned by the Pope, but when his coronation took place, Napoleon crowned himself instead.

Shaka

87 The first great chief of the Zulu nation in southern Africa was a warrior chieftain called Shaka (c. 1788–1828). He organized the army into regiments and gave his soldiers better weapons. Shaka made the Zulu nation the strongest in southern Africa.

88 Before Shaka, the Zulu people were relatively peaceful. Battles were often wars of words. Shaka changed all this, bringing in stabbing spears and training his warriors to destroy their enemies. He organized campaigns against neighbouring peoples, whom the Zulu either killed or forced to surrender.

89 Zulu boys practised fighting with sticks. At 18 they joined a regiment (*iButho*). Zulu warriors would sometimes fight duels with each other, swinging *iWisa* (clubs). It was seen as a way of making them tougher. In battle, they also used stabbing spears (*iklwa*), and throwing spears (*assegais*), and protected themselves with shields of cowhide.

▲ Shaka, the Zulu warrior chieftain. In the 1820s he ruled more than 50,000 people.

90 **Zulu regiments came together in a 'buffalo horns' formation.** New warriors formed the horns, experienced warriors made up the chest at the centre, and older fighters formed the body at the back. When they came within range, they threw their *assegais*. At close range, they used their stabbing spears.

91 **Shaka was murdered in 1828, but the Zulu fighting spirit lived on.** In 1879, the Zulu army fought the British in the Battle of Isandhlwana. The British had better weapons (rifles and bayonets), but the Zulu had more men, and they won a great victory.

▼ The British army was defeated by Zulus in the Battle of Isandhlwana (1879).

QUIZ

1. What did Zulu boys practise fighting with?
2. What were Zulu clubs called?
3. What was the Zulu battle formation called?

Answers:
1. Sticks 2. iWisa 3. Buffalo horns

Crazy Horse

92 **Crazy Horse (c. 1840–1877) was a Native American warrior chief.** He belonged to the Oglala Sioux people and was involved in a struggle with the US Army and white settlers. Crazy Horse wanted to stop them taking the Sioux land, and this led to a series of battles. He said he was 'hostile to the white man' and that the Sioux wanted 'peace and to be left alone'.

▲ A Sioux warrior could hang over one side of a galloping horse, using its body as a shield against the enemy.

◄ Crazy Horse was one of the greatest of all Native American war leaders.

93 **The traditional weapons of Sioux warriors were bows, lances and knives.** When they came into contact with white settlers, they began trading for rifles and pistols. However, weapons were not their most prized possessions – horses were. The Sioux used horses for hunting and for war. Their horses were small and fast, and the Sioux were expert riders.

QUIZ

1. Which native American tribe did Crazy Horse belong to?
2. What was a Sioux warrior's most prized possession?
3. In what year was the Battle of Little Big Horn?

Answers:
1. The Sioux 2. His horse 3. 1876

95 **From 1874, white settlers began moving into the Black Hills region of South Dakota, looking for gold.** This was the ancestral homeland of the Sioux. The US government ordered the Sioux to leave the area, but many refused to go. Crazy Horse called for Sioux warriors to fight, and they were joined by allies from the Cheyenne and Arapaho nations.

94 **As land was lost to white settlers, the Sioux began to act.** Warbands of warriors began to make hit-and-run raids against US Army outposts and isolated settlements. Stagecoaches and wagon trains carrying supplies were ambushed, and telegraph wires were cut. The US Army found these tactics very difficult to fight. It was as if the Sioux were an invisible enemy.

▼ The Battle of the Little Bighorn is also known as Custer's Last Stand.

96 **The US Army was sent to clear the area of Native Americans.** Crazy Horse and other leaders brought more than 1000 warriors together to resist them. On 25 and 26 June, 1876, the Battle of the Little Bighorn was fought near the Little Bighorn River, Montana. A force of 700 soldiers of the US Seventh Cavalry, led by General George Custer, was wiped out. Custer and a group of his men fought to the last on a small hill.

Fantasy warriors

97 Aragorn is a warrior in *The Lord of the Rings* trilogy of books, written by J R R Tolkien. He first appeared in 1954, in *The Fellowship of the Ring* and is the leader of a group of heroes tasked with destroying a ring of great power. During their quest, he has to fight evil creatures such as orks, goblins and the dreaded Nazgûl.

▼ Aragorn, as seen in the film version of the third book in the trilogy, *The Return of the King* (New Line Cinema, 2003).

98 Link is a fantasy warrior from the *Legend of Zelda* video games. He was created by Shigeru Miyamoto, and was 'born' in 1986. Link is portrayed as a brave warrior, who uses a magical sword, a boomerang, bombs and a bow.

99 **The Jedi are warrior knights from the *Star Wars* films.** Their role is to keep peace in the universe, by using the forces of good to defeat evil. They fight with lightsabers – energy swords of coloured light. The Jedi are organized into ranks. The most junior is a Jedi Youngling, and the most senior is a Jedi Grand Master.

▼ In the film *Star Wars Episode IV – A New Hope* (LucasFilm 1977) Jedi Master Obi-Wan Kenobi (left) and Darth Vader use their lightsabers in a duel.

100 **Wolverine is a superhero comic book character.** He first appeared in 1974. His skeleton is reinforced with adamantium – a super-strong metal that also forms his long claws, which can slice through metal and stone. He is a skilled fighter and his body heals itself with incredible speed.

▲ Wolverine is one of a group of heroes called the 'X-men' who use their super physical and mental powers to fight evil and protect ordinary people.

Weapons of war

101 **People have used arms and armour to hunt, defend themselves and attack other people for thousands of years.** Arms are weapons that are carried by a single person. Armour is something that is worn or carried to protect against injury. Early armour was made from wood or leather, and the first arms were made from wood or stone.

▼ At the battle of Lechfeld in AD 955 the Germans crushed the much larger army of Magyars. The Germans succeeded because they were wearing suits of mail armour and carrying new weapons.

The first arms

102 **Some of the first arms were made from stone.** The earliest humans lived hundreds of thousands of years ago. Archaeologists (scientists who study the remains of ancient humans) have found weapons made of sharpened stone that were made by these ancient people.

▲ This handaxe is made from a single piece of stone. It was held in the hand and used with a chopping motion.

103 **Early weapons were used for both hunting and fighting.** Archaeologists have found bones from cattle, deer and mammoths, and discovered that these animals were hunted and killed by ancient people using stone weapons.

▶ Around 75,000 years ago, spears were made from a stone point, which was attached to a wooden handle with leather straps.

104 **The first warriors did not use armour.** It is thought that early tribes of people fought each other to get control of the best hunting grounds or sources of water. These men may not have used armour, relying instead on dodging out of the way of enemy weapons.

105

Shields were an early form of defence. A thrust from a spear could be stopped by holding a piece of wood in the way. People soon began to produce shields made of flat pieces of wood with a handle on the back. Over the years, shields came to be produced in many different shapes, and from a wide range of materials including metal, wood and leather.

▲ By about 300 BC, the Celts of Europe were producing beautiful shields decorated with bronze and colourful enamel. Some, like this one found in London, may have been used in ceremonies.

▶ Flint is a hard stone that can be chipped and flaked into a wide variety of shapes to produce different types of weapons, such as these points or tips for arrows.

106

Spears were the first effective weapons. Many early spears consisted of a stone point mounted on the end of a wooden pole. With a spear, a man could reach his enemy while still out of reach of the opponent's hand-held weapons. The earliest known spears are 400,000 years old and were found in Germany.

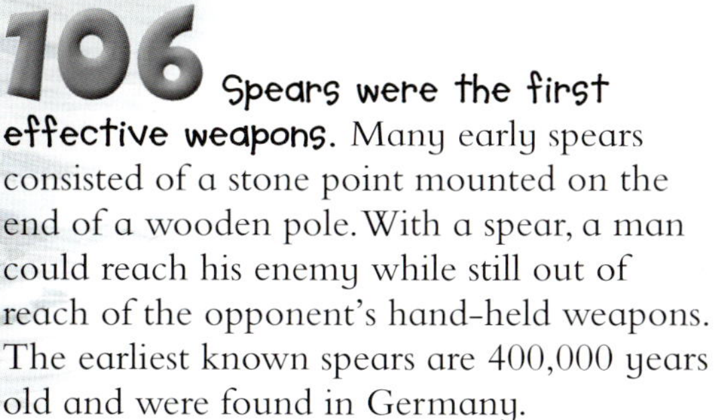

I DON'T BELIEVE IT!

The oldest signs of warfare come from Krapina, Croatia. Human bones over 120,000 years old have been found there that show marks caused by stone spearheads.

Ancient civilizations

▲ The Egyptian pharaoh Tutankhamun is shown firing a bow while riding in a chariot to attack the enemies of Egypt.

107 Early Egyptians may have used their hair as armour. Some ancient Egyptians grew their hair very long, then plaited it thickly and wrapped it around their heads when going into battle. It is thought that this may have helped protect their heads.

108 Some Egyptian soldiers had shields that were as big as themselves. Around 1800 BC, soldiers carried shields that were the height of a man. They hid behind their shields as the enemy attacked, then leapt out to use their spears.

109

Egyptian infantry (foot) soldiers often used axes. Soldiers that served as part of the bodyguard of the pharaoh (king) carried special axes. These weapons were made of bronze and each had a heavy round weight that meant they could deliver a heavier blow in battle.

▲ The curved blade of an Egyptian war axe. The weapon was able to crush any armour or shields in use at the time. This type of axe was used to cut, while other axes were used to pierce armour.

110

Assyrians wore long cloaks of mail. Some soldiers in the Assyrian army wore armour made entirely of mail around 900 BC. This was a series of interlocking metal rings that could withstand blows from swords or spears.

111

Babylonians wore armour that was brightly-coloured. Around 1000 BC, the ancient city of Babylon, Mesopotamia (now part of modern Iraq), was famous for its wealth. Babylonian soldiers wore armour that they often painted with bright colours to make themselves look more impressive in battle.

▶ An Assyrian army assaults a fortified city in Mesopotamia using siege towers and bows.

Hoplites and phalanxes

112 **Hoplites were armoured infantry.** From about 700 BC Greek infantry (foot soldiers) were equipped with a shield, helmet, spear and sword. They were called 'hoplites' ('armoured men'). Each hoplite used his own weapons and armour.

113 **A Greek who lost his shield was a coward.** The shield carried by hoplites was over one metre across and made of wood and bronze. It was very heavy, and anyone trying to run away from an enemy would throw it away, so men who lost their shields in battle were often accused of cowardice.

114 **Hoplites fought in formations called phalanxes.** When going into battle, hoplites stood shoulder to shoulder so that their shields overlapped, and pointed their spears forwards over the shields. A phalanx was made up of six or more ranks of hoplites, one behind the other.

▶ The success of Greek soldiers in battle depended on them keeping tightly in formation so that enemy soldiers could not get past the line of shields.

115

Greek spears had a 'lizard stabber'. Hoplite spears had a bronze spike at the bottom end. This was used to stick the spear upright into the ground and was called a 'sauroter', meaning 'lizard stabber'.

116

The best helmets were made from a single sheet of metal. Skilled metalworkers in the Greek city of Corinth invented a way to make a helmet by beating a single sheet of bronze into shape. This produced a helmet that was much stronger than one made of several pieces of metal. The helmets were called 'Corinthian'.

Roman legions

▲ A Roman legion marches out of a border fortress supervised by the legate, who commands the legion.

117 **Armoured infantry formed the legions.** The main fighting formation of the Roman army was the legion, a force of about 6000 men. Most were equipped with body armour, a helmet, a large rectangular shield, a sword and a throwing spear.

▶ The armour of a legionary was made up of several pieces, each of which could be replaced if it was damaged.

118 **Roman armour was made of metal strips.** At the height of the Roman Empire, around AD 50 to AD 250, legionaries wore armour called *lorica segmentata*. It was made up of strips of metal that were bent to fit the body, and held together by straps and buckles.

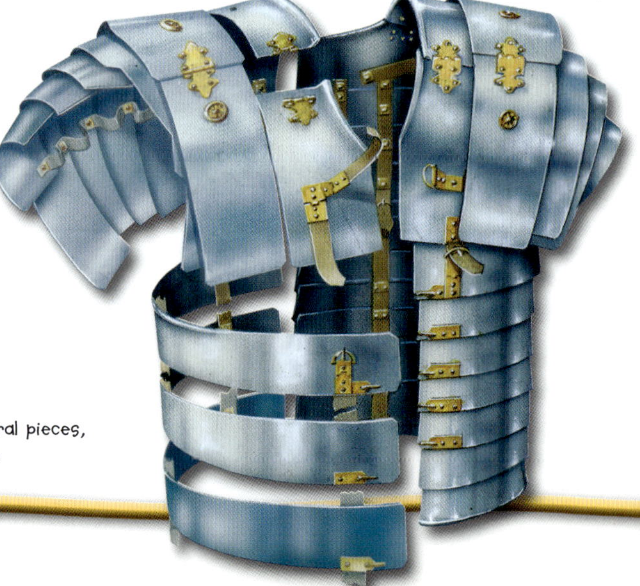

▶ In close combat, Roman soldiers used the gladius. It was a short sword, meant for stabbing rather than cutting.

▶ An auxiliary soldier wearing a short mail tunic and helmet, and carrying an oval shield. He has a gladius and javelin as weapons.

121 **Roman swords were copied from the Spanish.** After 200 BC, Roman soldiers carried swords with straight blades and sharp points. They were copied from swords used by Spanish soldiers who defeated the Romans in battle.

119 **Roman auxiliaries wore cheaper armour.** Every Roman legion included soldiers called auxiliaries (soldiers from places other than Rome). These units had to provide their own armour, often wearing tunics covered with mail or scale armour, which was made up of lots of small metal plates.

120 **Roman shields could form a 'tortoise'.** One tactic used by the Romans was called the 'testudo', or 'tortoise'. Soldiers formed short lines close together, holding their shields so they interlocked on all sides and overhead, just like the shell of a tortoise. In this formation they could advance on an enemy, safe from spears or arrows.

The fall of Rome

122 **Later Roman infantry abandoned armour.** By around AD 350, Roman legions preferred to fight by moving quickly around the battlefield. They stopped wearing heavy armour and relied upon large shields and metal helmets for protection.

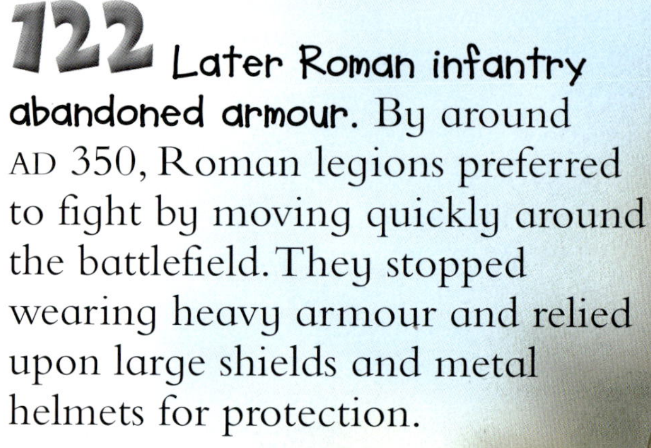

123 **Later Roman armies used mercenary archers.** Roman commanders found that archers were useful for attacking barbarian tribesmen. Few Romans were skilled at archery, so the Romans hired soldiers (mercenaries) from other countries to fight as archers in the Roman army.

124 **Roman shields were brightly coloured.** Each unit in the late Roman army had its own design of shield. Some were decorated with pictures of eagles, scorpions or dolphins, while others had lightning bolts or spirals.

◄ Late Roman shields were brightly decorated. Each unit in the army had its own design.

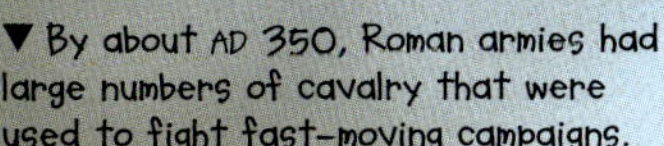

▼ By about AD 350, Roman armies had large numbers of cavalry that were used to fight fast-moving campaigns.

125

The eagle was a sacred standard. Each Roman legion had an eagle standard, the *aquila* – a bronze eagle covered in gold leaf mounted on top of a pole about 3 metres long. The *aquila* was thought to be sacred to the gods and it was a great humiliation if it was captured by the enemy.

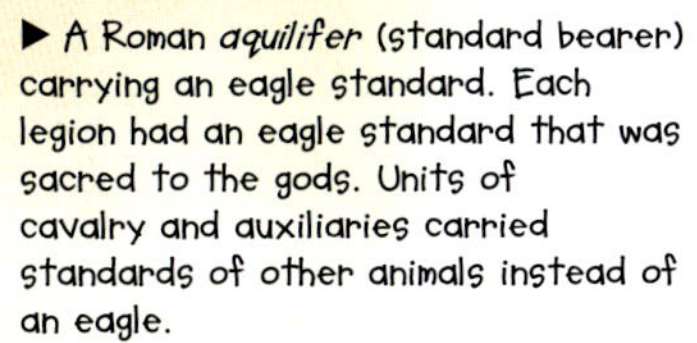

▶ A Roman *aquilifer* (standard bearer) carrying an eagle standard. Each legion had an eagle standard that was sacred to the gods. Units of cavalry and auxiliaries carried standards of other animals instead of an eagle.

126

Later Roman cavalry had enormous shields. One later group of Roman mounted soldiers was the *scutati*. These men wore coats of mail, and carried enormous shields with which they were expected to defend themselves and their horses. They would gallop towards the enemy army, throw javelins and then ride away before the enemy could strike back.

I DON'T BELIEVE IT!

Alaric the Goth and his men looted Rome in AD 410. Alaric was famously known to carry a sword with a handle made of solid gold.

Gladiators

127 **Gladiators fought in the arena.** Many Roman cities had a building called an arena, which had banks of seating and an oval area in the centre covered with sand. The arena was used to stage fights between men known as gladiators, who were trained to fight to the death to please the crowd. They used swords, spears, knives and other weapons when fighting.

128 **Gladiator helmets were large and decorative.** Fights were staged as part of an impressive show. The armour worn by gladiators was decorated with bright feathers, beautiful designs and may even have been coated with silver or gold leaf.

◀ Most gladiator helmets had metal masks to cover and protect the face.

▲ Samnite gladiators used a large shield and short sword, while Thracian gladiators had a small shield and curved sword.

129

Gladiator armour was not designed to save lives. The purpose of these fights was to put on a show of skill with weapons, and the penalty for defeat was death. If a gladiator was wounded in the arms or legs it was unlikely to kill him, but would mean an end to the fight. Some gladiators wore leg and arm armour so that the show could continue for as long as possible.

▶ A helmet worn by an andabata gladiator. It had no eyeholes so the wearer had to fight blind.

▲ The Retiarius was a type of gladiator based on a fisherman, so he carried a net and trident.

130

One type of helmet had no eyeholes. Sometimes gladiator show organizers would make the gladiators wear helmets called andabatae, which covered the eyes, so the gladiators had to rely entirely on their sense of sound.

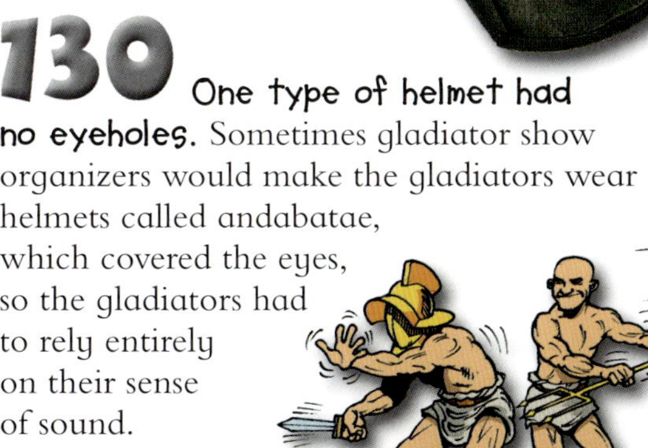

QUIZ

1. Which gladiators fought without being able to see?
2. Which types of gladiator carried a curved sword?
3. What was the name of the building where gladiators fought?

Answers:
1. Andabatae 2. Thracian 3. The arena

The Barbarians

131 **Celts used chariots to intimidate the enemy.** Battles between rival Celt tribes often began with famous warriors riding in chariots and performing tricks to show how skilled they were.

132 **The Huns were lightly equipped.** Around the year AD 370 the Huns swept into Europe from Asia. They fought on horseback with bows and spears, but wore no armour. They moved quickly, and showed no mercy.

133 **The Dacian falx was a terrible weapon.** The Dacians lived in what is now Romania around AD 400–600 and fought mostly on foot. Some Dacian warriors carried a long, curved sword with a broad blade that was called a falx. This weapon was so sharp and heavy that it could slice a person in half.

▶ The speed and accuracy of mounted Hun archers terrified the Romans.

134 **The Franks were named after their favourite weapon.** One tribe of Germans who lived around AD 300–600 were famous for using small throwing axes. These weapons had a short haft and a small, square-shaped head and were called 'francisca'. The men who used them were called franks, and soon the entire tribe took the name. They later gave the name to the country France.

◀ A Dacian warrior carrying a falx. Dacians were a people who lived outside the Roman Empire and often fought the Romans.

▼ A helmet belonging to an Anglo-Saxon king who ruled in East Anglia, England, about AD 625. It was made of iron and decorated with gold and silver.

135

Many barbarians wore armour decorated with gold, silver and precious stones. 'Barbarian' was the Roman name for uncivilized peoples outside the Roman Empire. They loved to show how rich they were and did this to emphasise their status within their tribe.

The Heavenly Kingdom

136 Chinese troops wore armour made of dozens of metal plates. The plates were about 8 centimetres by 6 centimetres and were sewn onto a leather garment or held together by leather thongs. Around 221 BC the various Chinese states were united. The Chinese believed this unity was the basis of their power and wealth.

137 Silk shirts helped protect against arrows. Many Chinese soldiers wore silk shirts under their armour. If an arrow pierced the armour it would drag the silk shirt into the wound without tearing it. By gently pulling on the shirt, the arrow could be extracted cleanly.

▼ A patrol of Chinese soldiers guarding the Great Wall around AD 200.

138 **Crossbows were first used in China.** They were more powerful than the bows used by nomadic tribesmen living north of China, so they were often used by troops manning the northern frontier. Crossbows consist of a short, powerful bow mounted on a wooden shaft and operated by a trigger.

139 **Infantry used pole weapons.** Chinese infantry often carried spears around 2 metres in length. Often an axelike chopping weapon, a slicing blade or a side spike replaced the spearhead. These weapons allowed the infantry to attack their enemies with a variety of actions to get around shields.

140 **Chinese cavalry were heavily armed.** When patrolling border regions, the Chinese cavalry operated in large formations that could defeat any tribal force causing trouble. The men were equipped with iron helmets and body armour, together with wooden shields and long lances tipped with iron.

QUIZ

1. In what year was China first united?
2. What did Chinese soldiers wear as protection against arrows?
3. Did the nomadic tribesmen live north or south of China?

Answers:
1. 221 BC 2. Silk shirts 3. North of China

The Dark Ages

141 **The Dark Ages followed the fall of Rome in AD 410.** Barbarian peoples took over the Western Roman Empire, and ancient culture and skills were lost. The Eastern Roman Empire lost power and lands to barbarians, but survived to become the Byzantine Empire. The Byzantines continued to use Roman-style arms and armour.

▲ English warriors patrol the great dyke built by King Offa of Mercia to define the border with Wales in AD 784.

142 **English cavalry were lightly armed.** Britain was invaded and settled by Germanic tribes from around AD 450, and by around AD 700 they ruled most of the island. Only the richest Englishmen wore body armour. Most went into battle armed with a spear and sword and carrying a round shield and a helmet as armour.

143 **Berserkers wore animal skins instead of armour.** Some Viking warriors were known as 'berserkers', meaning 'bear-shirts', from their habit of wearing bear or wolf skins in battle.

◄ A Viking berserker attacks dressed in a bear skin. These warriors would fall into a terrible rage in battle and seemed to ignore all danger.

144

The battleaxe was a terrible weapon. Many Scandinavian peoples used a battleaxe that had a haft up to 2 metres long and a blade more than 30 centimetres across. It was used with both hands. In the hands of a master, it could kill a horse and rider with a single blow.

QUIZ

1. Which warriors wore animal skins?
2. Who won the Battle of Lechfeld?
3. Who built a dyke between England and Wales?

Answers:
1. Berserkers 2. The Germans 3. Offa

◀ A Viking raiding party wielding battleaxes attacks a group of Englishmen.

145

The heavy cavalrymen ruled the battlefield. In AD 955 a small army of German knights destroyed the larger Magyar cavalry at the Battle of Lechfeld, in Germany. Knights (mounted men in armour carrying a spear and sword) were recognized as the most effective type of soldier.

Early knights

146 **The first knights wore mail armour.** Around the year 1000, most body armour in Europe was made of mail. This was flexible to wear and could stop a sword blow with ease. Such armour was expensive to make so only richer men could afford to wear it.

▲ Mail armour was made by linking together hundreds of small iron rings. The rings could be linked in a number of different ways, just like knitting a sweater.

147 **Shields were decorated to identify their owners.** From about 1150, knights wore helmets that covered their faces for extra protection. Around the same time, they began to paint heraldic designs (coats of arms) on their shields so that they could recognize each other in battle.

148 **Early knights sometimes used leather armour.** Mail armour was effective, but heavy and expensive, so some knights wore armour made of boiled, hardened leather. This was lighter and easier to wear, and was still some defence against attack.

◄ A knight in about 1100. He wears a shirt and trousers made of mail and a helmet shaped from a sheet of steel. His shield is made of wood.

149

Plate armour gave better protection than mail. By about 1300, new types of arrow and swords had developed to pierce mail armour. This led to the development of plate armour, made of sheets of steel shaped to fit the body, which arrows and swords could not easily penetrate.

150

The mace could smash armour to pieces. The most effective of the crushing weapons developed to destroy plate armour, the mace had a big metal head on a long shaft. A blow from a mace crushed plate armour, breaking the bones of the person wearing it.

QUIZ

1. Why did knights paint coats of arms on their shields?
2. How was leather armour treated to make it tough?
3. Which was the most effective crushing weapon?

Answers:
1. So that they could recognize each other in battle 2. It was boiled 3. The mace

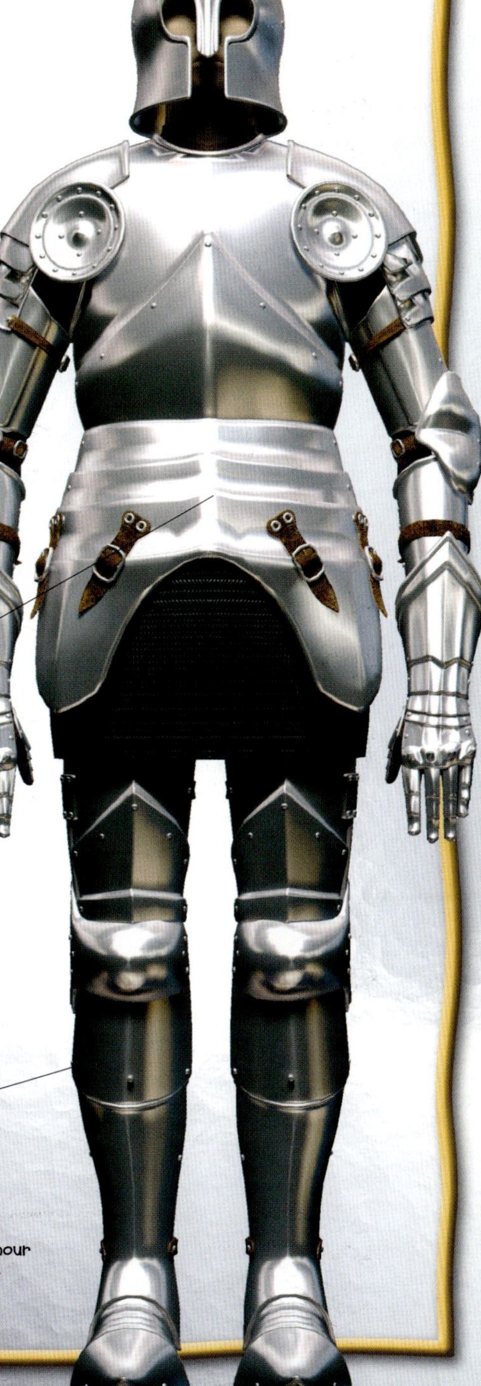

The armour around the stomach and groin had to be flexible enough to allow bending and twisting movements

The most complicated section of plate armour was the gauntlet that covered the hands. It might contain 30 pieces of metal

The legs and feet were protected by armour that covered the limbs entirely

▶ A suit of plate armour made in Europe in the early 14th century.

Archers and peasants

151 Infantry were usually poorly armed. Around 1000 years ago, ordinary farmers or craftsmen would turn out to protect their homes against an enemy army. Such men could not afford armour and usually carried just a spear and a large knife or an axe. They usually guarded castles and towns.

▼ A Welsh spearman in about 1350. He carries a spear and sword, but has no armour at all.

◄ An English archer in about 1400. He wears a metal helmet and has quilted body armour.

152 The longbow was a deadly weapon. From about 1320 the English included thousands of archers in their armies. The archers were trained to shoot up to eight arrows each minute, producing a deadly rain of arrows that could slaughter an enemy force at a distance.

153

Some weapons were based on farming tools. Many soldiers used weapons that were simply specialized forms of farming tools. The bill was based on a hedge-trimmer but could be used to pull a knight from his horse, and then smash through his plate armour.

▲ The heads of an English bill (left) and Dutch godendag (right). Both were pole weapons used by infantrymen.

154

Crossbows were used in some countries. Soldiers from Italy, the Low Countries (now Belgium and the Netherlands) and some other areas of Europe preferred to use the crossbow instead of the bow. It could not shoot as quickly, but was easier to learn how to use and much more powerful.

155

Some foot soldiers wore armour. Infantrymen sent to war by wealthy towns or cities were often equipped with armour. They usually formed solid formations with their long spears pointing forward, and could be highly effective in battle.

◀ A crossbowman would hide behind a large shield called a pavise while reloading his weapon.

Make a castle bookmark

You will need:
card   scissors   crayons   sticky tape

1. Draw a tower 12 centimetres tall on card and cut it out.
2. Draw the top half of a soldier holding a shield on card and cut it out.
3. Colour in the tower and soldier.
4. Place the soldier so that his body is behind the tower and his shield in front.
5. Tape the soldier's body to the back of the tower to hold it in place.

Your bookmark is ready to use!

Later knights

156 Armoured knights were the most important troops. Knights had the best arms and armour and were the most experienced men in any army, so they were often put in command.

157 Knights sometimes fought on foot, instead of on horseback. English knights fought on foot after about 1300. This enabled them to hold a position more securely and co-operate more effectively with other soldiers.

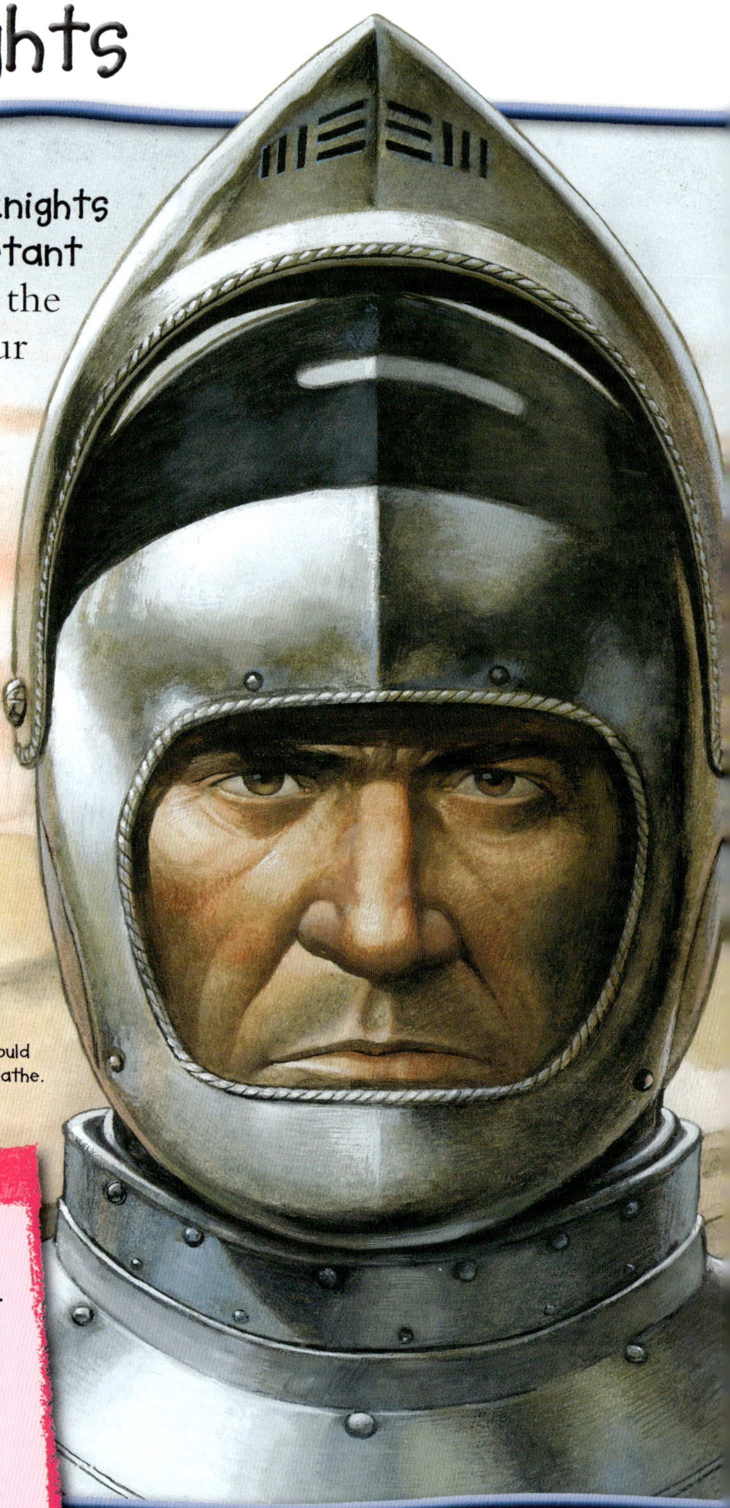

▶ The bascinet helmet had a visor that could be lifted so the wearer could see and breathe.

I DON'T BELIEVE IT!

At the Battle of Agincourt in France in 1415, the English killed 10,000 Frenchmen, but only about 100 Englishmen lost their lives.

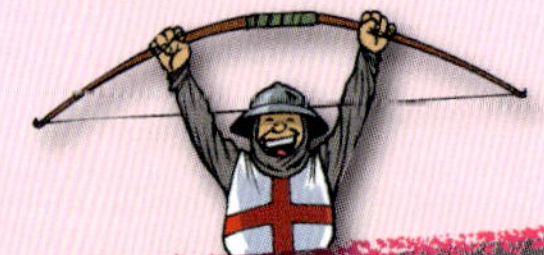

158

Horse armour made of metal and leather was introduced to protect horses. By about 1300, knights began to dress their horses in various sorts of armour. Horses without armour could be killed or injured by enemy arrows or spears, leaving the knight open to attack. Men with armoured horses were put in the front rank during battle.

▶ Horse armour was shaped to fit the horse's head and neck, then was left loose to dangle down over the legs.

159

The flail was a difficult weapon to use. It consisted of a big metal ball studded with spikes and attached to a chain on a wooden handle. It could inflict terrible injuries, but also swing back unexpectedly, so only men who practised with it for hours each day could use it properly.

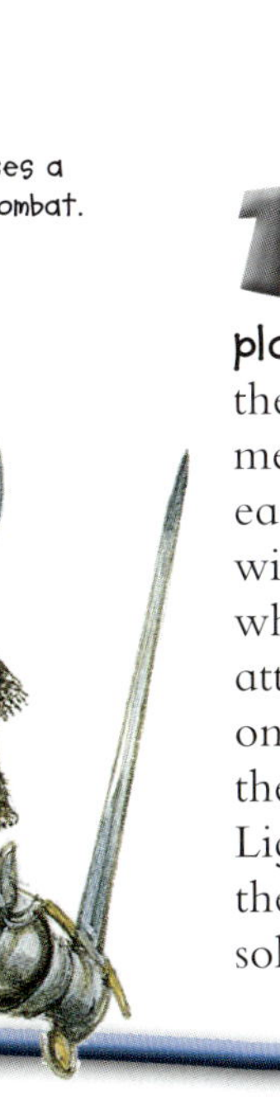

◀ A knight uses a flail in foot combat.

160

Each man had his place in battle. Before each battle, the commander would position his men to ensure that the abilities of each were put to best use. The men with the best armour were placed where the enemy was expected to attack, while archers were positioned on the flank (left or right side) where they could shoot across the battlefield. Lightly armoured men were held in the rear, ready to chase enemy soldiers if they began to retreat.

Desert warfare

161 Bows were made of many materials. In the desert areas of the Middle East, soldiers used bows made from layers of animal horn, bone and sinew that were stuck tightly together and then carved into shape. These were called 'composite bows', and fired arrows with much greater force than longbows.

▲ The recurved bow was short, but powerful.

162 The Mongols wore light armour. A tribe from central Asia called the Mongols were led by Genghis Khan (1162–1227). Their armour was light because there was a lack of iron in Central Asia. As a result, they developed tactics based on fast-moving cavalry attacks.

163 **Curved swords were known as scimitars.** Armourers working in the city of Damascus, Syria, invented a new way to make swords around the year 1100. This involved folding the steel over on itself several times while the metal was white hot. The new type of steel was used to make curved swords that were both light in weight and incredibly sharp, called scimitars.

164 **Teneke armour was made up of a mail coat onto which were fixed overlapping pieces of flat metal.** These pieces were about 6 centimetres by 2 centimetres. The plates were loosely hinged so that air could pass through easily but blows from a sword could not. The armour was light, comfortable and effective, but it was also expensive.

▲ A Saracen wearing teneke armour and wielding a scimitar. The Saracens wore flowing cloaks and turbans to help combat the heat of the desert.

◄ A Mongol army attacks men from the city of Kiev, Ukraine. Although designed for grasslands and deserts, Mongol weaponry was effective in cold forests as well.

165 **Armour was light because of the desert heat.** The plate armour in use in Europe was not worn in the deserts of the Middle East. The plates of metal stopped air circulating around the body and were very uncomfortable to wear. Instead desert fighters in the 13th to 15th centuries wore loose robes and light pieces of armour.

Indian arms

166 India had a unique tradition of arms manufacture. Between 1650 and 1800 the vast lands south of the Himalayas, modern India, Pakistan and Bangladesh, were divided into lots of small states. Each state had its own army, and made great efforts to have impressive weapons.

167 The khanda was a sword with a long, straight blade. These swords had heavy, double-edged blades that often had handles big enough to allow them to be held in both hands. Larger khanda were slung from a belt over the shoulder so that they hung down the user's back.

168 Indian soldiers used the pata. This was an iron glove (gauntlet) that extended almost to the elbow, attached to a sword blade. It was very useful for thrusting, especially when attacking infantry from horseback, but was less effective at cutting.

169

Talwars were curved swords with a single, sharp cutting edge. The handles were often rounded, rather like the butt of a pistol. They were highly decorated with silver, gold and semi-precious stones.

▲ The talwar sword was invented around AD 1000 and was used in battle for over 900 years.

170

Elephants were used in warfare. A small platform, ('howdah'), was strapped to the back of the elephant. Men armed with bows, or later with guns, sat in the howdah and shot at the enemy over the elephant's head.

▶ War elephants were often covered in armour, while the howdah, in which the soldiers sat, could be covered with iron.

Island wars

171

Polynesians fought without armour or shields. The islands in the Pacific Ocean were home to people of the Polynesian culture. Before contact with Europeans around 1750, the Polynesians made their weapons from natural materials. They preferred to rely on skill and movement in battle rather than armour, though some men wore thick shirts of plaited coconut fibres as protection.

172

Shark teeth were made into swords. In western Polynesia, shark teeth were added to the sides of long clubs to produce a weapon called the tebutje. This was used to cut as well as smash and was a vicious close-combat weapon.

▼ A Polynesian war canoe on its way to a raid on another island. The warriors paddling the canoe kept their weapons beside them.

▲ Boomerangs often had decorative carvings or were brightly painted.

173
The boomerang didn't always come back. Native Australian people used spears and bows and arrows, as well as the boomerang. This heavy throwing stick was shaped so that it spun round in the air and could be thrown with accuracy. Only the lighter boomerangs, used for hunting birds, were designed to come back to the thrower.

174
War clubs were favoured weapons. Wooden clubs were carved from single pieces of wood and were over one metre in length. They had wide, heavy heads that were often elaborately carved with shapes and patterns.

▶ A Maori mere, or short club. These weapons were made from very hard woods.

175
The Maori used wooden weapons. The Polynesian people who live in New Zealand are known as the Maori. They produced unique types of club. One type was the mere, which had a short handle and a wide curved blade that could be used for slashing at the enemy.

African arms

176 **The iklwa was a deadly weapon.** The Zulu nation of southern Africa was ruled by King Shaka from 1816–1828, who built up an empire covering thousands of square kilometres. Shaka introduced a new weapon, the iklwa, a short spear with a broad blade used for stabbing. It proved more deadly than the traditional throwing spears used by other peoples in the area.

177 **Assegai were throwing spears.** They had smaller and lighter heads than the iklwa. Zulu warriors would begin a battle by throwing their two or three assegai. Then they would run quickly forward to attack with their iklwa.

178 **Helmets were for show, not defence.** Zulu warriors wore headdresses to make them look tall and impressive. They were made of wickerwork with tall ostrich feathers, flowing crane feathers and strips of coloured fur or woollen tufts attached.

179

Knobkerries could crush skulls.
Many Zulu warriors carried a heavy wooden club,
or knobkerrie, as well as the iklwa. If the iklwa was
lost, the knobkerrie could be used for close fighting.

180

Shields were made of cowhide. Zulu shields were nearly
2 metres in length, and were cut
from cowhide, which was laced
onto a central wooden pole
with strips of leather.

Make Zulu puppets

You will need:
card   ice-lolly sticks
crayons   glue

1. Draw some Zulu warriors onto card.

2. Cut out each of the warriors and colour them in.

3. Glue an ice-lolly stick to the back of each warrior.

4. If you make enough Zulus, glue the lolly sticks to a straight piece of wood so that the warriors form a rank.

◀ A Zulu impi, or army, on the march. Boys
followed the warriors carrying bedding, food
and spare weapons.

The Americas

181 In South America, spears were thrown at the start of a battle. The Aztec people built up a large empire in what is now Mexico between 1400 and 1510. Their warriors won a series of battles against other American peoples. Each battle began with men on both sides throwing light javelins at the enemy. Then the men would charge at each other to fight at close quarters.

◄ In battle, some Aztec warriors dressed as eagles, jaguars and other fierce animals.

182 Obsidian stone was razor sharp. The Aztec, Maya and other peoples of South America did not know how to make iron or bronze, so they made their weapons from natural materials. The most effective weapons were edged with slivers of obsidian, a hard, glasslike stone that has a very sharp edge when first broken.

183

Clubs were used to knock enemies unconscious. One of the main purposes of warfare among the Maya and Aztec people was to capture prisoners. The prisoners were then taken to temples to be sacrificed to gods such as Huitzilopochtli, the god of war, by having their hearts cut out while still beating.

184

Shields were highly decorated. The shields used by Aztec and Maya warriors were made of wood, and covered with brightly coloured animal skins and feathers. They often had strings of feathers or fur dangling down underneath to deflect javelins.

◀ The Maya tried to capture enemy noblemen and rulers to use as sacrifices to the gods.

185

The tomahawk was a famous weapon of the North American tribes. This was a short-handled axe with a heavy head. The first tomahawks were made with stone heads, but after Europeans reached North America, the tribes began buying steel-headed tomahawks.

▶ The native peoples of the eastern areas of North America used spears and special axes, known as tomahawks.

The code of Bushido

186 Samurai wore elaborate armour. From around 800–1860, warriors known as the samurai ruled the islands of Japan. Samurai wore suits of armour made from hundreds of small plates of metal laced together with silk. Each group of samurai had a badge, or sashimono, which was often a picture of a plant or animal.

187 The swords of the samurai took weeks to make. The samurai sword was produced by blending strips of different types of steel, and shaping them to produce a smooth blade. Each sword was made by a master craftsman in a process that involved prayers and religious rituals as well as metalwork.

188 Bushido was the way of the warrior. By around 1500 the samurai were expected to follow a code of behaviour known as Bushido, which demanded loyalty and honour as well as bravery and skill with weapons.

▲ The samurai practised with weapons and armour for long periods. They sometimes exercised with elaborate displays.

Make Sashimono flags

You will need:
A4 coloured paper   scissors
string   crayons

1. Fold each piece of paper in half.
2. On both sides of each piece of paper draw an animal or plant.
3. Hang each piece of paper over the string at the fold to make a line of flags.
4. Hang the flags up in your room.

▲ All samurai were trained in mounted combat and were expected to use their bows as well as their swords when riding at a gallop.

189 Archery was a great skill.

Around AD 800, the earliest samurai called their profession 'the path of the arrow'. This was because skill at archery was thought to be the most important for a warrior. Swords later became more important, but archery remained a key skill until the end of the samurai period in the 1860s.

190 Most samurai carried two

swords. The katana was most often used in combat, while the shorter wakizashi was used in an emergency or for ritual suicide. Some samurai preferred the much longer two-handed nodachi sword when going into battle.

▶ A print of a samurai warrior showing the brightly patterned clothes that the warriors liked to wear.

The end of an era

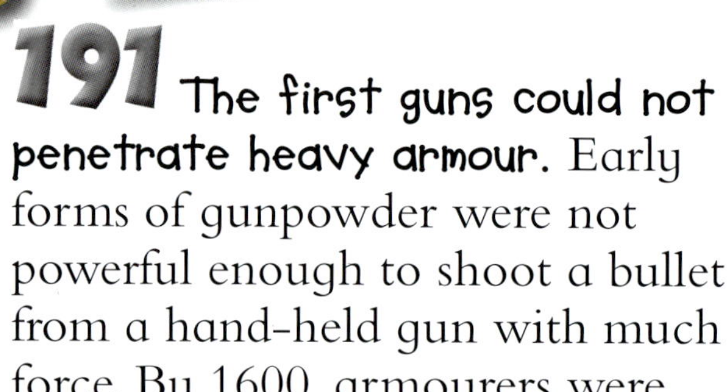

191 **The first guns could not penetrate heavy armour.** Early forms of gunpowder were not powerful enough to shoot a bullet from a hand-held gun with much force. By 1600, armourers were producing helmets and breastplates that were bulletproof.

193 **Cavalry continued to wear body armour.** Until 1914, cavalry engaged in fast-moving fights could often not reload their guns once they had been fired. As a result cavalrymen often fought using swords and lances, so armour was still useful.

192 **Cannons could destroy armour.** Large cannons fired iron or stone balls that weighed up to 25 kilograms. They were designed to knock down stone walls, but were also used in battle. No armour could survive being hit by such a weapon.

▼ A French cavalryman in 1810. He wears an iron helmet and iron body armour.

194

Infantry officers wore gorget armour. This was one of the last kinds of armour to be worn. It was a small piece of armour that fitted under the front of the helmet and protected the neck. Gorgets were often used to show the rank of the man wearing them, so they continued to be worn long after helmets were abandoned. They were used until 1914 in some countries.

▶ A musketeer in about 1770. He is using a ramrod to push the bullet and gunpowder down the barrel of a gun before firing it.

195

By 1850 most soldiers no longer wore armour. As guns became more effective, they were able to fire bullets with greater accuracy over longer distances and with more power. By 1850 most infantry were armed with guns that could shoot through any type of armour, so most soldiers stopped wearing armour.

I DON'T BELIEVE IT!

As late as 1914 some French cavalry went to war wearing armour, despite the fact that they had to face artillery and machine guns.

Modern arms and armour

196 **The first modern use of chemical weapons was in World War I.** In April 1915, the Germans used poison gas against French soldiers. It worked by irritating the lining of the lungs and throat. Soldiers then began to wear anti-gas uniforms as protection.

▶ A British infantryman in 1944. He wears a steel helmet and carries a Sten gun — a light machine gun.

▲ A British cavalryman charges in 1916. Both the man and horse wear gasmasks to protect them against poison gas.

197 **Modern soldiers always wear helmets.** Exploding shells and rockets often throw out sharp splinters of metal called shrapnel. Soldiers take cover in trenches or holes. Metal helmets protect the head, the most likely part of the body to be hit by shrapnel.

▶ A Main Battle Tank (MBT) advances through the desert. The arrival of tanks and other armoured vehicles has transformed modern warfare.

198 Modern armoured warfare involves tanks.

The armour needed to stop modern shells and rockets is too heavy for a person to carry, but it can be mounted on a vehicle, such as a tank or an armoured personnel carrier (APC). These vehicles are the key feature of a modern army, as the armoured knights were in the middle ages.

199 The best armour makes you disappear.

Camouflage conceals soldiers by using colours that blend into the background of plants, sky or sand. Helmets often have a strap that can be used to attach vegetation for extra camouflage.

▼ An American soldier in Iraq. He wears bulletproof body armour as well as a helmet.

200 Bomb disposal soldiers use special armour.

Designed to give protection against blast waves, the armour covers as much of the body as possible while still allowing the soldier to use his hands to defuse the bomb.

Warriors of Japan

201 **For hundreds of years, there was a group of warriors in Japan known as samurai.** Their name means 'someone who serves'. All samurai served a warlord (military leader) and battles were fought between armies of rival warlords. Samurai followed a set of rules called *bushido*. These rules told them how to behave, not just in battle, but in everyday life. Respected members of Japanese society, the bravest and fiercest samurai became well-known figures.

▼ Samurai armies fought at close range, on foot and on horseback. This scene shows the Battle of Kawanakajima in 1561, in the north of the main Japanese island of Honshu.

From emperor to shogun

202 **Japan is an island country in the Pacific Ocean, located off the coast of mainland Asia.** It is made up of four main islands (Hokkaido, Honshu, Shikoku and Kyushu) and nearly 4000 smaller ones. The islands are mountainous, with forested slopes and fast-flowing rivers. There are many active volcanoes, including the famous Mount Fuji.

▲ Japan is a nation of many islands that lie close together. It has had several capital cities over the years.

QUIZ

1. Which family took power away from the emperor?
2. Who was the first emperor of Japan?
3. What is the name of Japan's most famous volcano?
4. Which was the first permanent capital of Japan?

Answers:
1. The Fujiwara family 2. Jimmu 3. Mount Fuji 4. Nara

203 **Japan was once ruled by emperors.** Legend says that the first emperor was Jimmu, who reigned in 660 BC. Early emperors had great power. Then about AD 800 they became 'figurehead rulers'. This meant that they were still heads of state, but had little power.

DATE	PERIOD	NOTABLE EVENTS
14,000–300 BC	Jomon	• Early people are hunter-gatherers and decorate clay pottery with distinctive patterns
300 BC–AD 300	Yayoi	• Farmers begin to grow rice in paddy fields
AD 300–710	Kofun	• Buddhism is introduced to Japan
AD 710–794	Nara	• Nara becomes the first permanent capital city
794–1185	Heian	• Kyoto becomes the capital city
1185–1333	Kamakura	• Battle of Dan-no-Ura • Minamoto Yoritomo becomes the first shogun
1333–1573	Muromachi	• Members of Ashikaga family become shoguns. They are finally driven out by the warlord Oda Nobunaga
1573–1603	Azuchi-Momoyama	• Oda Nobunaga is succeeded by Toyotomi Hideyoshie • Japan is reunited
1603–1868	Edo	• Japan isolates itself from the rest of the world • US Commodore Matthew Perry forces the Japanese government to open up ports for trade
1868–1912	Meiji	• Japan becomes modernized and grows to be a world power

▶ Japanese history is divided into several periods. These are often named after the most powerful family, or the site of the capital city at that time.

204

In about AD 800, power was taken from the emperor. It fell into the hands of the Fujiwara clan. They were a noble family that had married into royalty, and for about 300 years they were the real rulers of Japan. However in the 1100s, the Fujiwaras lost control after a bitter war. From then on, power passed to military dictators called shoguns.

206

Japan's first permanent capital city was Nara, on the island of Honshu. It became capital in AD 710 and the emperor lived there. In AD 794, Kyoto was made the new capital and home of the emperor. Tokyo, which was known as Edo until 1868, is the present-day capital.

205

Shogun means 'commander of the forces'. He was a military dictator – the person in control with unlimited power. In 1192, Minamoto Yoritomo became the first shogun. He was known as the 'barbarian-conquering great general'.

▶ Minamoto Yoritomo, the first shogun. Shoguns controlled Japan until 1867.

Religion and ritual

207 Japanese society was divided between rich and poor.

A few rich families owned all the land and the poor owned none. The poorest people worked on the land, and had to pay taxes to the powerful landowners. This type of system is known as feudalism. Japan was a feudal society for hundreds of years.

▶ At the top of Japanese society was the emperor, even though he had no real power. Merchants were the lowest class.

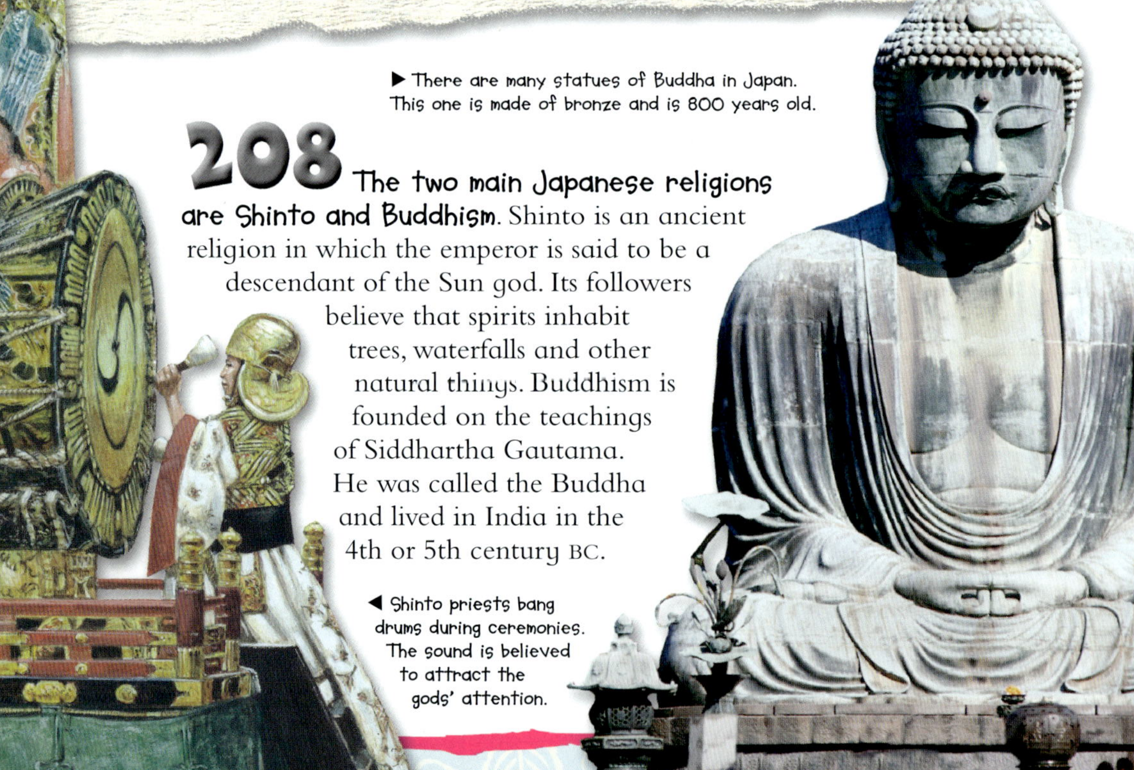

▶ There are many statues of Buddha in Japan. This one is made of bronze and is 800 years old.

208 The two main Japanese religions are Shinto and Buddhism.

Shinto is an ancient religion in which the emperor is said to be a descendant of the Sun god. Its followers believe that spirits inhabit trees, waterfalls and other natural things. Buddhism is founded on the teachings of Siddhartha Gautama. He was called the Buddha and lived in India in the 4th or 5th century BC.

◀ Shinto priests bang drums during ceremonies. The sound is believed to attract the gods' attention.

210

Before battle, a samurai warrior might visit a Shinto shrine. A priest would give him a small cup of *sake* (rice wine) to drink, and the soldier would offer prayers to a god. In return for his prayers, the soldier hoped the god would protect him. Samurai had favourite gods to pray to, such as Taira Masakado (see pages 16–17). After he died, in AD 940, he was believed to have become a god.

◀ Shinto shrines were important places of worship. Samurai visited them to pray for good fortune.

209

Ancestors were special. If a samurai had heroes among his ancestors, he showed them respect by displaying their names at his family altar. It was a way of keeping their memories alive, and the warrior hoped he would inherit their bravery and courage.

211

Rituals were very important. These were set ways of doing ordinary things. During the 1400s, samurai began to carry out the tea ceremony. This was an elaborate way of making and enjoying a cup of tea. The tea was made by carrying out steps in a precise order.

▼ Equipment used during the tea ceremony. The ritual is linked to Buddhist ideas of tranquility (calmness).

Hishaku (water ladle)

Kama (iron pot used to heat the water)

Mizusashi (container containing cold water)

Chashaku (tea scoop)

Chasen (bamboo whisk)

Chaki (dry tea leaf container)

Chawan (tea bowl, used for drinking)

The first samurai

▶ A samurai warrior of the AD 900s. Mounted warriors were especially skilled at using the bow and arrow.

212 **The first samurai appeared in the AD 900s.** They were warriors who belonged to the private armies of Japan's noble families, or clans. The clans owned large amounts of land, which they needed to protect from rivals. The best way to do that was to build up an army of soldiers in case of battle.

213 **Samurai protected their bodies with armour.** The first samurai wore armour made from small iron or leather scales, laced together with silk or leather cords. The scales were arranged into separate sections, each of which was designed to protect a different part of the samurai's body.

214 **In the early years of the samurai, the soldier on horseback was the elite warrior.** He was an archer, and fired arrows from a bow as his horse galloped along at speed. The mounted archer practised his archery techniques over and over again. In battle, when he had fired all his arrows, an archer fought with a sword.

215 Infantry (foot soldiers) were lower class fighters. It was their job to hold up their shields to protect the mounted archers, who were seen as the main fighting force. As well as defending the horsemen, the infantry were also responsible for disrupting the enemy by setting fire to their property.

▲▶ Each clan had its own mon, or family crest. It was used on flags, and helped soldiers to identify their comrades.

216 The two leading clans were the Minamoto (also called the Genji) and the Taira (also called the Heike). They were bitter rivals whose armies fought battles against each other to decide which was the leading clan.

Let battle begin!

217 **An argument between rival clans would often lead to a battle.** When the two sides faced each other on the battlefield, the armies followed a strict sequence of events. The battle began with archers firing arrows that made a whistling sound. The noise was believed to be a sign to the gods, asking them to protect the samurai who were about to fight. It was also a scary sound for the enemy.

218 **It was an honour to be first into battle.** A man was chosen from among the mounted warriors. He was picked because he was a champion fighter and came from a long line of warriors. Facing the enemy, he named his ancestors and listed his achievements in battle. It was a challenge to the other side to send out a warrior of equal status.

219

An opponent from the rival army would ride out to meet his enemy. The two men then fought a duel on horseback, firing arrows at each other as they rode at speed around the battlefield. It was a contest to show who was the best rider and the best archer.

220

If the archery duel didn't produce a winner, the two men began hand-to-hand combat. They dismounted from their horses, and fought until one of them was killed. The winner cut off his opponent's head and presented it to his commander as proof of his courage and skill. After the duel, fighting broke out. Men fought one to one, in groups, on horseback and on foot.

▲ In hand-to-hand fighting, samurai fought with swords that had long, curved blades.

I DON'T BELIEVE IT!

The mounted archer Minamoto Tametomo described how his arrow went straight through his opponent's saddle, passed through his body, then came out the other side!

221

The element of surprise was one of the most effective fighting tactics. Soldiers would try to catch their foes off-guard and ambush them, or creep up to their buildings and set them on fire.

Taira Masakado

222 **Born around AD 903, Taira Masakado is the first samurai commander that historians know much about.** Part of the Taira clan, Masakado was the great-great grandson of Emperor Kammu. In his youth he served at the court of the Fujiwara clan in the capital Kyoto. The Fujiwaras were Japan's rulers at the time.

223 **The Taira clan had its origins in AD 825, when the surname Taira was given to a branch of the royal family.** The Taira settled in Hitachi, a district northwest of present-day Tokyo. They became the ruling family of the region, and built up a private army.

224 **Masakado wanted the Fujiwaras to appoint him as head of the national police.** The Fujiwara clan refused to do this, so Masakado left their court and moved to the Kanto district of central Japan. From there, he lead a war against the Fujiwara clan. In AD 939 he conquered districts in eastern Japan and proclaimed himself as the new emperor.

▼ Taira Masakado knocks a foot soldier to the ground. In old pictures such as this, he is always shown as a brave warrior.

226 In Kyoto, Masakado's head was put on a platform. Legend says the head flew back to Masakado's base in Kanto. From there it went to Shibasaki, where it was buried with honour. Today, that place is known as Masakado Kubizuka (the Hill of Masakado's head), in Tokyo. Masakado is seen as a hero who fought the government for the rights of ordinary people.

▼ At the Hill of Masakado's Head, there is a shrine in honour of Taira Masakado.

225 The government sent an army to defeat Masakado, who they regarded as a rebel. This army was led by Taira Sadamori. The two sides clashed at the Battle of Kojima, in AD 940, and Masakado was killed in the fighting. His head was cut off and sent to the emperor in Kyoto as proof of his death.

▼ The Battle of Kojima took place during a gale. Wooden shields erected by Masakado's army were blown down.

Minamoto Yoshiie

227 **The Minamoto clan was an offshoot of the Japanese royal family.** But in the AD 800s it was decided that none of them would be emperor. They were given the surname Minamoto and moved from the capital at Kyoto to a new base at Osaka, in southern Japan. Here they became the district's ruling family.

228 **Minamoto Yoshiie was a samurai commander.** He turned the Minamoto clan into a major fighting force. Born in 1039, at Kawachi, in the district of Osaka, his father was a samurai leader, and Yoshiie learned all the skills of the warrior from him.

◄ Minamoto Yoshiie was one of the greatest samurai commanders.

▶ Yoshiie earned the title *Hachiman-Taro*, meaning 'son of the god of war'.

229

Yoshiie's first battles were against the Abe clan. He fought alongside his father to defeat them in a war that raged for about nine years, and ended in 1062. The Minamoto clan took control of much of north Japan, with Yoshiie as ruler. Twenty years later, he defeated the Kiyowara clan, who had started to challenge him. The Minamotos were the undisputed rulers of north Japan.

I DON'T BELIEVE IT!

Once, Yoshiie guessed that his enemy was about to ambush him in a surprise attack because he saw a flock of geese suddenly fly out of a forest.

230

After each battle, Yoshiie spoke to his troops. Men who had shown the most courage were invited to sit on a 'bravery' seat. All of them wanted this honour. None wanted to sit on the other 'cowardice' seat. To be called a coward was a disgrace.

231

Yoshiie's victories made him the greatest general in Japan. He made Kyoto his home, and he hoped the government would reward him with a position of power, but they never did. Yoshiie spent his last years living quietly in the capital, where he died in 1106.

▼ A bronze statue of Minamoto Yoshiie in Fukushima, on the island of Honshu.

The Gempei War

232 **As Japan's clans became stronger, a power struggle began.** The greatest conflict was between the Taira and Minamoto clans, who clashed in a series of battles known as the Gempei War, fought between 1180 and 1185. Both clans were related to Japan's royal family, and they wanted to control it — and the rest of Japan.

233 **The Gempei War began when Taira Kiyomori ordered the death of Minamoto Yoritomo.** Kiyomori and Yoritomo were the leaders of their respective clans. At first, the Taira forces were successful, and Yoritomo's army was heavily defeated. But the war was not over.

▶ Minamoto Yoritomo (1147–1199) led the Minamoto clan during the Gempei War.

▼ In 1180, Minamoto Yoritomo sent one of his men to kill an enemy from the Taira clan. It marked the start of the Gempei War.

234 **The Taira clan had a reputation for being harsh.** As the war progressed, Taira troops started to defect and join the Minamoto army. It was now the Minamoto's turn for battle honours. In 1183, the Minamoto army seized the capital at Kyoto, then attacked the last strongholds of Taira resistance, which were in western Japan.

SAMURAI SYMBOLS

Every samurai clan had its own *mon* (see page 99). This was a symbol that was easy to recognize. *Mons* were usually based on plants or simple patterns made from dots, curves and lines. Some were based on animals, but these were less common. What *mon* would you design for your family? Look at the *mons* in the pictures in this book to give you some ideas.

235 **The final action of the Gempei War was the sea battle of Dan-no-ura, in 1185.** Warships of the Taira and Minamoto clans fought in the narrow strip of water between the islands of Honshu and Kyushu. When it was clear the Minamoto would win, many of the Taira threw themselves into the sea.

236 **By 1192, the Minamoto clan controlled Japan.** That year, Minamoto Yoritomo visited the emperor in Kyoto. The emperor appointed him as the first shogun (military dictator). From then on, Japan had two rulers – the god-like emperor (who had little power) and the shogun, the most powerful person in the land. It was a system that lasted until the mid–1800s.

▼ The Taira clan were defeated at the Battle of Dan-no-ura. This scene shows Taira Tomomori tied to an anchor, about to drown himself.

Bushido — the samurai code

237 **Samurai followed a code of behaviour known as *bushido*.** It means 'the way of the warrior'. *Bushido* was a set of rules that governed all aspects of a samurai's lifestyle. It demonstrated that a samurai was an educated and refined man with knowledge of the arts and literature – as well as being a brutal killer who would slice off his enemy's head without hesitation.

▼ As well as being fierce warriors, samurai were required to be well dressed and educated.

238 **A samurai was expected to be a confident warrior.** He had to believe he was strong, not just hope that he was. Self-belief was a key part of *bushido*. If warriors had doubts in themselves it meant they were weak, and weakness was not 'the way of the warrior'.

◀ A samurai was expected to show confidence at all times, and believe he was a worthy warrior.

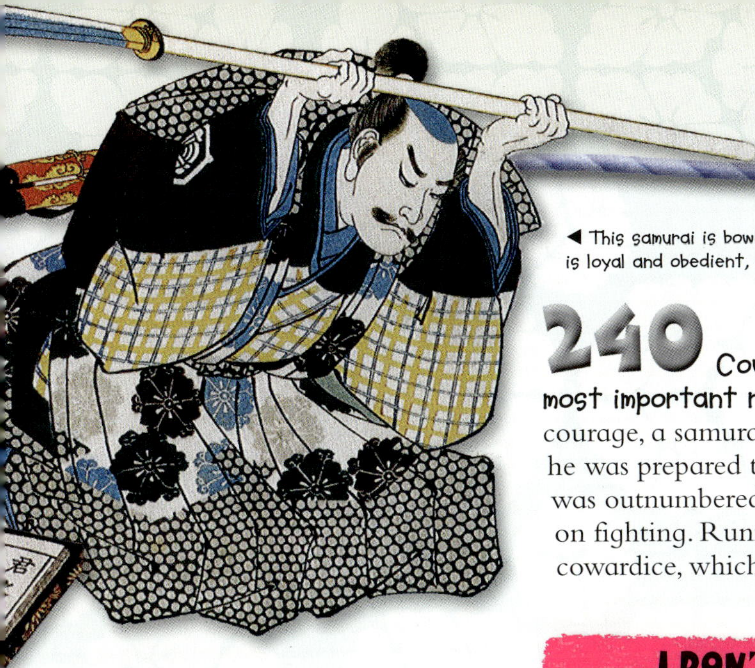

◀ This samurai is bowing to his master, showing he is loyal and obedient, a key part of *bushido*.

240 Courage was one of the most important rules of *bushido*. To show courage, a samurai had to demonstrate that he was prepared to fight to the death. If he was outnumbered in battle, he had to carry on fighting. Running away was a sign of cowardice, which was punished.

239 Showing loyalty to the warlord was another rule of *bushido*. The warlord gave orders, and samurai obeyed them without question. By obeying orders, samurai showed obedience.

I DON'T BELIEVE IT!

Samurai were told to be careful when chasing their enemies. If an enemy got too far ahead, he could easily turn around and charge, putting the attacking samurai in danger.

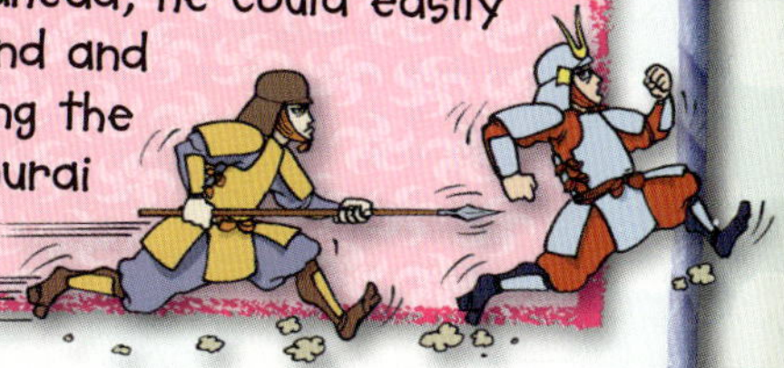

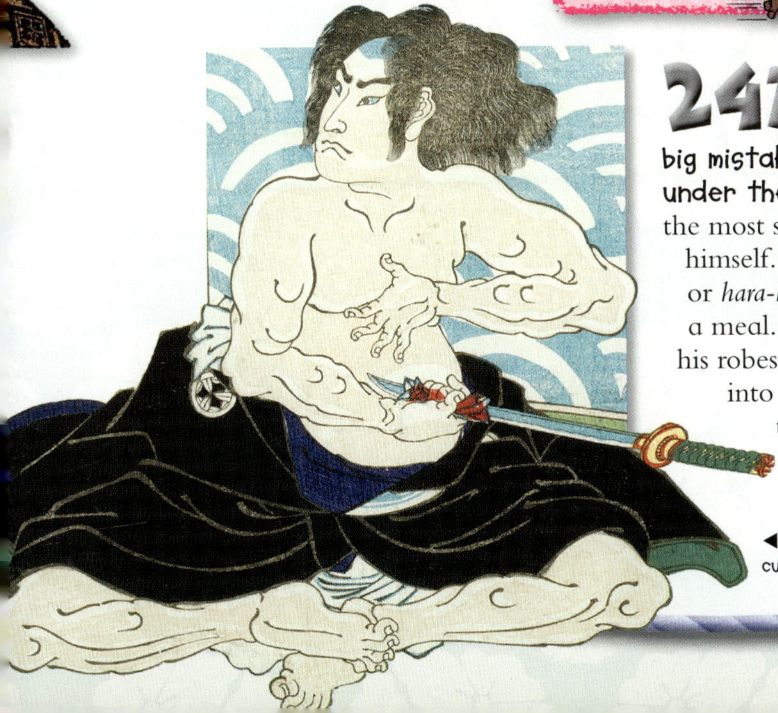

241 If a samurai made a big mistake, he was punished under the rules of *bushido*. In the most serious cases, he would kill himself. This was called *seppuku*, or *hara-kiri*. The samurai first ate a meal. After this he opened up his robes and plunged a dagger into his stomach. As he did this, another samurai cut his head off with a swing of his sword.

◀ A samurai about to commit *seppuku*, cutting open his own stomach.

Samurai armies

242 By the 1550s, Japan was divided into many states, each of which was ruled by a *daimyo*. He was the warlord and head of a clan. Rival clans were almost constantly at war with each other. To protect their territory, warlords had large armies. As fighting increased, the armies grew more organized.

244 Foot soldiers were called *ashigaru*. They made up a large part of a warlord's army, and there were always many more *ashigaru* than mounted samurai. *Ashigaru* fought with swords, spears, bows and *naginata* (see page 115). From the 1540s they began to use guns called arquebuses.

243 Armies clashed during the fighting season, which lasted from spring until the end of summer. No fighting took place during the harvest season, which began in September, or in winter. Most foot soldiers were peasants from farming communities, and when it was harvest time they returned to their homes to gather crops.

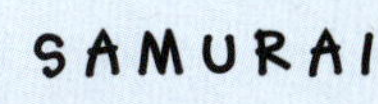

245

A samurai army was divided into units of men. The elite troops were always the men on horseback. The *ashigaru* were organized into groups of spearmen, archers and arquebusiers (soldiers with firearms). Other groups of *ashigaru* carried flags and banners, and some were given the job of carrying the army's baggage.

246

On the battlefield, generals controlled troop movements by waving fans. The fans had swinging tassels on them, making the fan movements easy to see. Sound signals were another way of sending information to the troops, such as blowing on conch shells and beating on drums and gongs.

▼ A samurai army on the march. *Ashigaru* foot soldiers are flanked by mounted samurai. The most powerful clans had armies of over 100,000 men.

Warrior training

247 **Boys were taught to be warriors.**
They began school at about the age of seven,
and for the next five or six years
were taught to read, write and
play musical instruments.
From about the age of ten,
they were taught to fight.
When a boy reached
13, he had a coming-
of-age ceremony,
and from then on
he was ready to
fight in battle.

▶ Boys were taught to
fight using sticks, but
these would eventually
be replaced with swords.

248 **Some clans set up
military training schools, or *dojo*.**
Here, boys were taught martial arts by
trainers, or *sensei*. The *sensei* were skilled
in the use of weapons, and had served in
samurai armies. It was their job to pass
these essential skills on.

249 **Mounted warriors were
the elite troops of a warlord's army.**
Their main weapon was the bow, and
they had to fire arrows at moving targets
as their horses raced at speed. They
practised by firing arrows at running
dogs. At the start of training, most
arrows missed, but eventually they
would learn when to release an arrow
to hit a moving target.

251 Women married to samurai were trained to fight.

Although their main work was to look after the family, there was always a chance that an enemy raiding party might attack the family home. To fight off attackers, women used daggers and *naginata* (see page 115). Some warlords had bands of armed women patrolling the grounds of their castles.

▲ When using dogs as target practice, the horsemen used blunt arrows. It was not their intention to kill the dogs.

250 In another type of target practice, mounted samurai fired arrows at targets fixed to poles.

They rode along a course, and as they moved past a small wooden board they fired an arrow. There were three targets, and the archer only had three arrows. The most skilful samurai made each arrow count and hit each target.

▶ Tomoe Gozen (c. 1157–1247) was a female warrior who fought on the side of the Minamoto clan during the Gempei War.

Weapons with edges

252 Swords were the main edge weapons used by samurai. The blades were made of steel, in a process that involved heating and folding the metal several times. A sword was seen as the 'soul' of a samurai. The finest swords were made by master swordsmiths. They carved their own names, the names of the owners, and good luck verses on the sword handles.

Hilt or handle (*tsuka*)

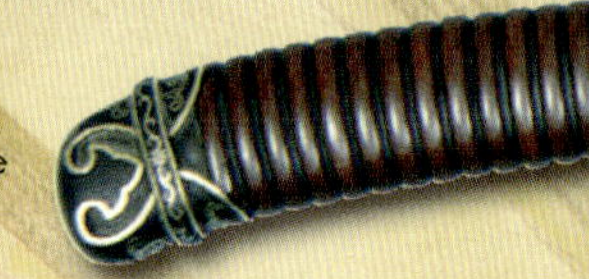

253 New swords were tested for sharpness. They were tried out on sheaves of straw wrapped around bamboo, oak poles, copper plates and even metal helmets. Sometimes they were tested on people too, and were used to behead criminals. The best swords were so sharp they could cut through several bodies placed on top of one another.

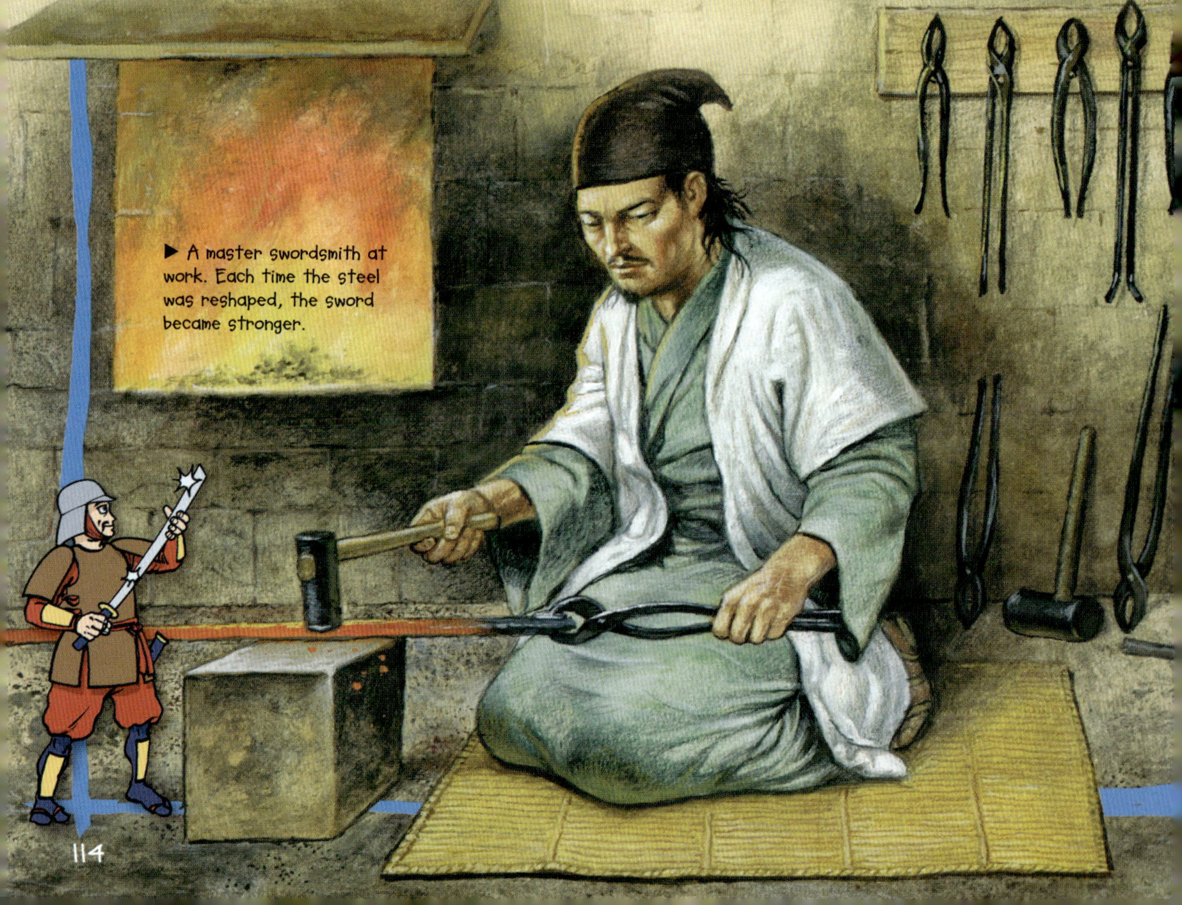

▶ A master swordsmith at work. Each time the steel was reshaped, the sword became stronger.

Scabbard (*saya*)

Guard (*tsuba*)

Point of blade
(*kissaki*)

254

The main fighting sword was called a *katana*. It had a long, curving blade and was mainly used for combat on foot. The samurai held his sword in both hands as he moved it in a series of attacking strokes, from zigzags and circles to up, down and diagonal slashes. He could also use it on horseback, holding it with one hand, not two.

▲ A short sword or *tanto* and its scabbard. Like the *katana*, the *tanto* was incredibly sharp.

◄ The curved blade at the end of a *naginata*.

256

Samurai used other weapons with sharp edges. The *naginata* was a long pole with a curved metal blade at the end. The blade was used for slashing, and the pole for beating. It was mainly a weapon of the *ashigaru*, who also used stabbing spears.

▲ Each *katana* was highly prized. The best swords were given names, such as 'The Monster Cutter' or 'Little Dragon'.

▲ Guards at the end of the hilt (handle) of a *katana* stopped the swordsman's hand from slipping onto the blade.

255

Short swords called *tanto* were used for fighting at close quarters. Every samurai carried a *tanto*. It was often the stabbing thrust of a *tanto* that decided the outcome of a duel. The victorious samurai then cut off the loser's head.

▶ Most spears had pointed tips. Some were hook-shaped and used to drag men from their horses.

Missile weapons

257 **The bow was as important to the samurai as the sword.** It was called a *yumi*, and was almost 2.5 metres in length. Made from strips of wood and bamboo, it fired arrows to a distance of about 380 metres, but its killing range was no more than about 80 metres.

▶ Arrowheads came in different shapes and sizes to carry out different functions.

Armour-piercing arrowheads

258 **Arrows were made of bamboo, and there were many types of arrowhead.** Some made whistling noises, some had armour-piercing tips, and some had forked heads to cut through ropes. One legend says a samurai archer sank an enemy ship by firing an arrow through its hull below the waterline.

Forked arrowhead

Whistling arrowhead

Match (rope for burning)

◀ The longbow was an effective weapon, and samurai archers were highly trained.

259

In siege warfare (attacking a castle or city), samurai armies used machines to hurl stones. The first stone-throwers were giant crossbows but these were eventually replaced by trebuchets, a type of catapult. Trebuchets were used to bombard enemies with heavy rocks, which shattered when they hit the ground, causing casualties and damage.

▼ Samurai soldiers prepare to hurl a rock from a trebuchet.

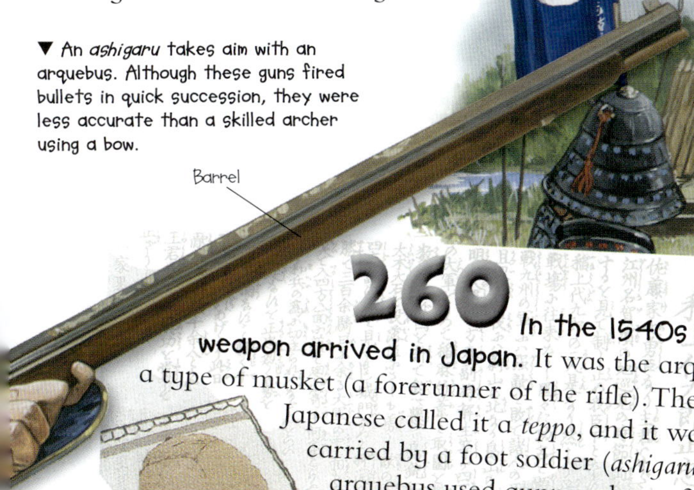

▼ An *ashigaru* takes aim with an arquebus. Although these guns fired bullets in quick succession, they were less accurate than a skilled archer using a bow.

Barrel

260

In the 1540s a new weapon arrived in Japan. It was the arquebus, a type of musket (a forerunner of the rifle). The Japanese called it a *teppo*, and it was carried by a foot soldier (*ashigaru*). The arquebus used gunpowder to fire a lead ball over a distance of about 500 metres, with a killing range of about 200 metres.

261

Another gunpowder weapon was the cannon. However, unlike the arquebus, which was widely used, the cannon was not very popular with samurai armies. Any cannon that were used came from Dutch and English ships that visited Japan.

◄ This soldier is using a large bore arquebus, which fired a big lead ball.

Amazing armour

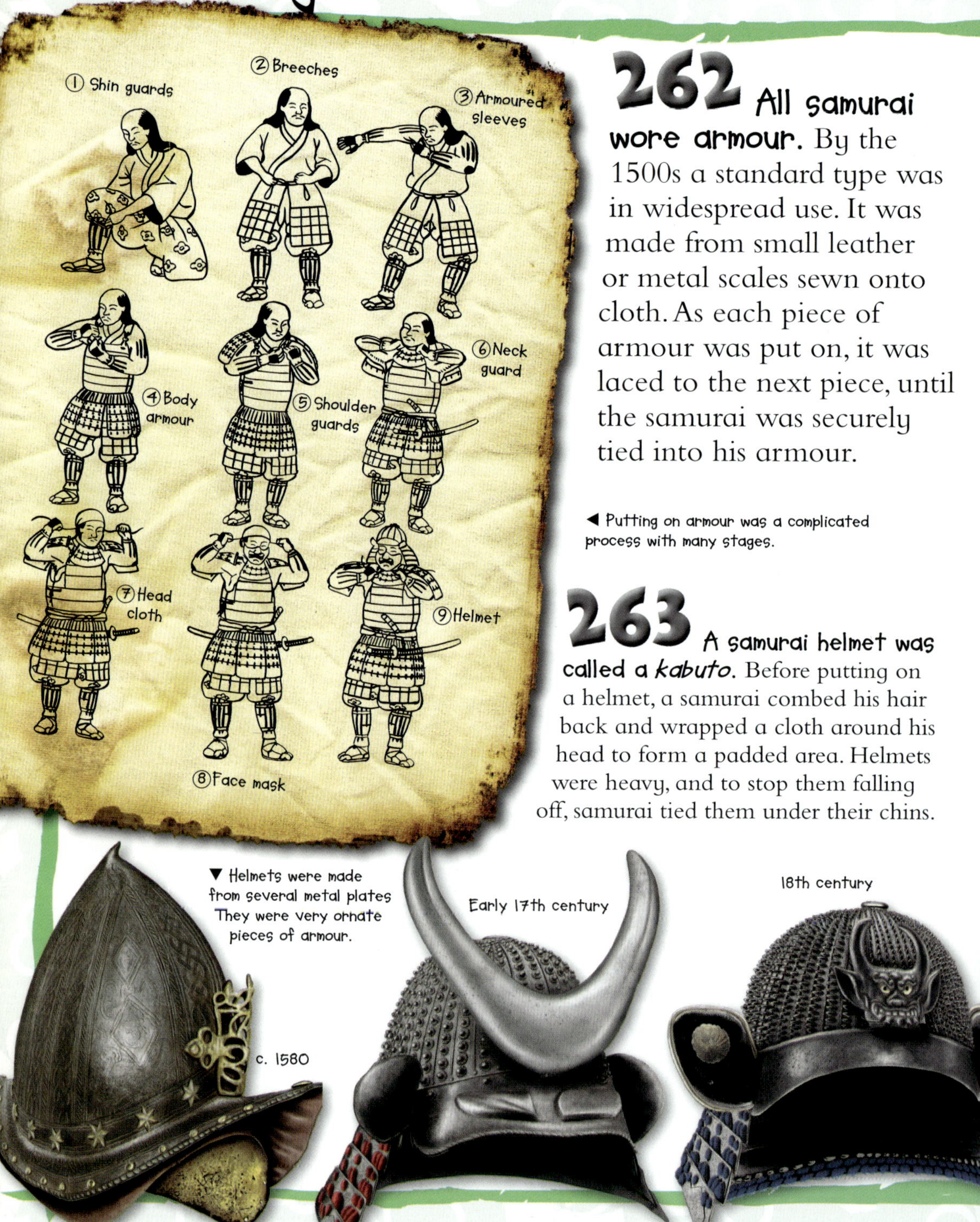

◄ Putting on armour was a complicated process with many stages.

▼ Helmets were made from several metal plates. They were very ornate pieces of armour.

262 **All samurai wore armour.** By the 1500s a standard type was in widespread use. It was made from small leather or metal scales sewn onto cloth. As each piece of armour was put on, it was laced to the next piece, until the samurai was securely tied into his armour.

263 **A samurai helmet was called a *kabuto*.** Before putting on a helmet, a samurai combed his hair back and wrapped a cloth around his head to form a padded area. Helmets were heavy, and to stop them falling off, samurai tied them under their chins.

264

Most samurai went into battle barefaced, but some wore a face mask, or *mempo*. This could cover the whole of the face, or just the chin, cheeks, mouth and nose. The mask was usually painted, and the mouth was shaped like a grimace so the warrior looked as if he was snarling.

▲ Some masks had bristling fake moustaches to make the wearer seem even more terrifying.

265

Samurai armour could be brightly coloured. Lacquer (varnish) was painted over each piece. It not only made the armour stand out, it also made it hard-wearing. The five 'lucky' colours were red, blue, yellow, black and white.

▶ Eighteenth century armour from the Edo Period.

266

Samurai of the Li clan in the 1500s were known as the Red Devils. Their armour was coated with red lacquer, making them instantly recognizable. They chose red to make themselves appear more frightening, and because no other clan wore this colour.

Clothes and food

267 For everyday clothing a samurai wore a *kimono*. This was a long, wide-sleeved gown that came to below his knees and was kept in place by a belt wrapped around the waist. He wore a pair of *hakama* (wide trousers) under the *kimono* and socks and sandals on his feet. His *katana* (sword) was tucked into his belt.

▶ A samurai in everyday dress. Even though he was not fighting, he still carried his sword.

◀ A samurai with a typically shaven head. His remaining hair was tied in a bun at the back.

268 Tidy hair was important. It was considered a disgrace if a man let his hair become untidy. In the 1500s, samurai began shaving the hair from the front part of their heads. This made it more comfortable to wear a helmet in battle. Hair at the sides and rear of the head was combed back and tied into a bun.

269 **Rice was the staple food in Japan.** It was eaten boiled and steamed, and as rice cakes and rice balls. Fish, pork, boar and rabbit were the main meats eaten. When samurai went to war, most warriors took portions of rice with them. If they raided an enemy camp or village, they took the enemy's food supplies.

◄ A local farmer offers a samurai commander baskets of melons for his troops. Fruit was popular with soldiers on campaign.

270 **Before a battle, samurai shared a meal together.** It was a way of bringing the warriors closer to each other in the last few hours before fighting began.

271 **A helmet was not just for wearing.** Some foot soldiers (*ashigaru*) used their metal helmets as cooking pots! They turned them upside down and boiled rice inside them over a fire. Small groups of men probably took it in turns to cook for their comrades.

► An *ashigaru*'s metal helmet had two functions – protective armour and a cooking pot to boil rice.

Castle fortresses

272
To protect their territory, samurai clans built castles. Some were built on flat plains, but most were built on mountains. Their purpose was to defend key areas such as bridges, river crossings, roads and mountain passes.

▶ A castle was surrounded by a strong wall. Inside were courtyards, each of which could be closed off if intruders broke through the main defences.

273
Castles built in the 1500s were heavily defended. At the centre was the keep – the tallest and grandest building within the castle grounds, where the *daimyo* (warlord) lived. If intruders broke through the castle's outer line of defence, they were faced by a series of walls with gates that took them into open courtyards – where they could be easily attacked.

274 **A clan's most important castle was the home of the *daimyo*.** Around this castle were the homes of generals and family members. The more important the person was, the closer to the leader's castle they were allowed to live. A town grew up around the castle. Rice was grown in the surrounding fields to provide food for the townspeople.

275 **Matsumoto Castle is one of Japan's finest samurai castles.** It was built in the late 1500s, on a flat plain in central Japan. Its location made it an easy target, but the builders protected it with three moats and strong ramparts. The castle complex was surrounded by an earth wall 3.5 kilometres in circumference. The only way to enter or leave was through two heavily fortified gates.

276 **Castles were difficult to attack.** Armies besieged a castle until its occupants surrendered. When Takamatsu Castle was besieged in 1582, the attackers diverted a river until it formed a lake. As the lake grew, it flooded the castle, and the occupants gave in. The defeated leader rowed out on the lake and committed suicide (*seppuku*).

KEY

① Keep (where the *daimyo* lived)
② Moat
③ Outer wall
④ Inner wall
⑤ Gatehouse

The age of battles

277 Many battles took place all over Japan in the years 1450–1600. This time is known as the Warring States Period. It was a time of civil war, when rival states attacked each other, trying to win territory. The battles were fought on a large scale, and from the mid-16th century arquebuses were used – the first time this deadly firearm was put into practise in a big way.

278 Armies fought in battle formations. Generals decided which formation was best to use, and the troops moved into place. Formations had names such as 'birds in flight', 'keyhole' and 'half moon'. In the 'birds in flight' formation, the arquebusiers protected the archers, who fired arrows over the heads of the musketmen. The general was at the centre, surrounded by his warriors.

Birds in flight formation

Keyhole formation

Half moon formation

▼ Three different types of battle formation. Every man knew his place and was expected to keep to it.

279

The 'arrowhead' formation was used to break through enemy lines. Arquebusiers fired their muskets, opening up gaps in the enemy's front ranks. When the gaps were big enough, samurai rushed past their gunmen, and through the gaps. Hand-to-hand fighting followed using swords, daggers, *naginata* and spears.

◀ The arrowhead formation takes its name from the pointed arrow-like position of the troops.

281

The greatest prizes were the heads of the losers. They were cut off and presented to the general for him to inspect. First, the heads were washed, the hair was combed, and they were placed on spikes on boards. Labels attached to the hair gave the names of the dead, and the names of the men who had killed them.

280

After the battle, the victors took the spoils. The dead of both sides were stripped of their weapons and armour. Scavengers from nearby villages helped themselves to whatever they could carry. Wounded warriors were of no use to anyone. They were killed by local villagers, who then took their belongings.

▼ The severed head of an enemy soldier being presented for inspection.

I DON'T BELIEVE IT!

If the eyes of a severed head were closed, it was a lucky sign. If they were open and looking upwards, it was an unlucky sign.

Oda Nobunaga

282 One of greatest samurai commanders of the Warring States Period was Oda Nobunaga. He was born in 1534, and became *daimyo* (warlord) of the Oda clan when he was just 16. Because he was so young, rival clans thought they could easily overpower his army and take his land – but they were wrong. In a series of battles, Nobunaga's forces defeated his enemies.

284 The Battle of Nagashino was fought in 1575. In this great battle, Nobunaga sent an army to the castle of Nagashino. The castle was besieged by an army from the Takeda clan. Nobunaga's plan was to end the siege by fighting the Takedas.

283 Nobunaga's rise to power began in 1560. In that year, his territory was invaded by the Imagawa clan. The Imagawa army was 12 times the size of Nobunaga's, and they quickly took several of his fortresses. It looked as if Nobunaga would be defeated. But, during a thunderstorm, Nobunaga mounted a surprise attack. The Imagawa *daimyo* was killed, and Nobunaga's territory was saved.

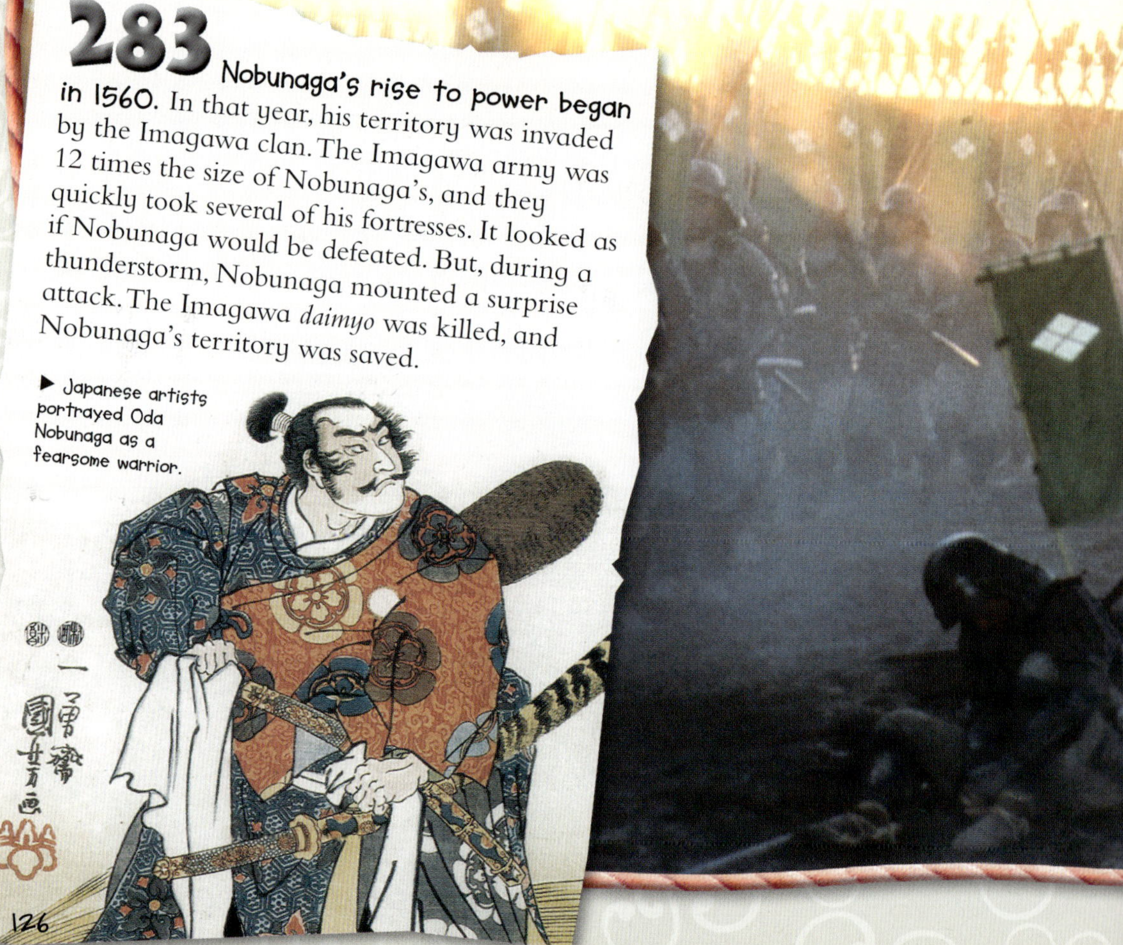

▶ Japanese artists portrayed Oda Nobunaga as a fearsome warrior.

285

The Nobunaga and Takeda armies clashed on a plain near Nagashino Castle. Mounted samurai from the Takeda clan charged at Nobunaga's forces, and were felled by shots from as many as 3000 arquebusiers. A second wave of Takeda horsemen swooped down, by which time the musketmen had reloaded. After hours of bitter fighting, the Takeda army withdrew.

QUIZ

1. How old was Nobunaga when he became leader of his clan?
2. What was the weather like when Nobunaga defeated the Imagawa daimyo?
3. How many arquebusiers did Nobunaga use against the Takedas?
4. When was the Battle of Nagashino?
5. In which city did Nobunaga die?

Answers:
1. 16 2. There was a thunderstorm 3. 3000 4. 1575 5. Kyoto

▼ A scene from *Kagemusha*, a film released in 1980. Set during the Warring States Period, it ends with the Battle of Nagashino.

286

Oda Nobunaga died in 1582. He had become the most powerful general in Japan, and acted as if he was the country's shogun. This made him many enemies. On a visit to Honnoji Temple, in Kyoto, he was attacked by his own men. Some accounts say he died in the attack, others say he was captured and forced to commit *seppuku*.

Flags and standards

287 **Samurai carried flags and standards into battle.** There could be hundreds of flags fluttering in the wind on the battlefield, and each one had its own meaning. Some were decorated with family, clan or religious symbols, others had messages on them. It was the job of an army's foot soldiers to carry the flags.

288 **A battlefield could be a confusing place.** In the rush of horses and the scattering of men, it was easy for a soldier to become separated from his fellow warriors, or lose sight of his *daimyo* (warlord). If this happened, all he had to do was look around for the flags of his own side, which he recognized by their familiar symbols.

▼ ► The red umbrella great standard of Oda Nobunaga and the golden bell great standard of Mukai Tadakatsu, leader of the Omura clan.

▲ The Soma-Nomaoi Festival is held each year in Haramachi City. Here, horsemen in traditional samurai armour parade with flags decorated with clan symbols, or *mons*.

289 **In samurai battles of the late 1500s and 1600s, the *daimyo* had two standards.** They were the 'great standard' and the 'lesser standard', both were mounted on long poles. A standard was an important object to a clan. Not only was it instantly recognizable, it represented what the clan stood for, and was to be protected.

291 **Samurai could attach flags to their backs.** These were called *sashimono*. The shaft of the flag slotted into a holder in the armour, leaving both hands free for weapons. *Sashimono* were often decorated with the clan's colours or symbols. Some samurai painted their flags with messages, giving the name of the wearer and the name of the man he hoped to kill in battle.

▶ A *sashimono* attached to the back of a samurai. 'Leader' is written on his flag in Japanese.

290 **It was a great honour to be a standard-bearer, but this honour brought danger.** The enemy was drawn towards the other side's standard, so the standard-bearer was always in the thick of the fighting. The defending army would do everything they could to save the standard from being captured. If the standard-bearer fell, another man quickly took his place.

DESIGN A FLAG

Have a close look at the flags pictured in this book, then design one of your own. Note how the flags are long and thin, which made them easy to carry. Keep your design simple and bold, and use strong colours so that it really stands out.

Samurai in decline

292 **On 21 October 1600, the Battle of Sekigahara took place.** It was fought between the armies of Tokugawa Ieyasu (with 80,000 men) and Ishida Mitsunari (100,000 men). An estimated 30,000 men died on the battlefield. The Tokugawa clan won, and the battle brought an end to the Warring States Period.

293 **Tokugawa Ieyasu became shogun in 1603.** It was the start of a relatively peaceful period in Japan's history that lasted for the next 250 years. In 1639, Japan became a 'closed country'. It was forbidden to have contact with foreigners, and Japanese people were not even allowed to leave the country.

▼ The arrival of the American navy in Tokyo harbour in 1853 caused great concern in Japan.

294

The clans were now at peace with each other, and their armies were disbanded. The idea of going to war to steal another clan's territory became a thing of the past. Samurai traditions and rituals still carried on, but they were performed for peaceful purposes.

▼ Emperor Meiji ruled Japan from 1868 to 1912.

295

In 1853 and 1854, a fleet of ships from the USA arrived in Tokyo Harbour. The American fleet was led by Commodore Matthew Perry. His aim was for Japan to stop being a closed country and to open up to foreign trade. The Tokugawa clan were still Japan's rulers, and the shogun Tokugawa Iesada decided to open up the country. Many Japanese thought this was a bad thing.

296

Japan's system of an emperor sharing power with the shogun came to an end in 1867. It was a system that had lasted for 675 years. The last shogun, Tokugawa Yoshinobu, handed power back in 1867, and in 1868, Emperor Meiji became the sole ruler of Japan. For some people, these changes were too much to bear.

The last samurai

297 **The Satsuma Rebellion took place in 1877.** Samurai were unhappy at the changes in Japan. For centuries they had been respected, and feared, members of society. Gradually their way of living had changed, and now they felt out of place as Japan began a process of modernization, bringing to an end centuries of feudal rule. When they were told to lay down their swords, it was the final insult, and a rebellion began.

▶ Saigo Takamori (1828–1877), leader of the rebel forces during the Satsuma Rebellion, was the last samurai commander.

298 **Leader of the rebellion was Saigo Takamori.** His army of 40,000 samurai fought against a larger government force. The samurai fought with their traditional weapons – the sword and the bow. The Japanese army fought with rifles.

▲ Soldiers of the Japanese army with rifles (left) clash with samurai armed with *naginata*.

299 **The rebellion lasted for about eight months.** It ended at the Battle of Shiroyama, on 24 September 1877. Takamori's forces had been reduced to a few hundred men. He was heavily outnumbered, but refused to surrender as this was against the *bushido* code. Takamori was wounded, and then he committed *seppuku* rather than face being captured. His remaining men were cut down by gun fire.

300 **Many films have been made about the samurai.** The most famous is *Seven Samurai*, made in Japan in 1954 and set in the Warring States Period. Another is *Kagemusha*, made in 1980. Both of these films were directed by Akira Kurosawa, who is regarded as the greatest samurai film-maker of all time. Hollywood has also made films about samurai, such as *The Last Samurai* in 2003 with Tom Cruise in the title role.

▼ In the 2003 Warner Brothers' film *The Last Samurai*, actor Tom Cruise plays the part of an American fighting on the side of the samurai during the Satsuma Rebellion.

I DON'T BELIEVE IT!

In the *Star Wars* movies, the costume of Darth Vader was inspired by samurai armour.

Castle life

301 **A castle was both a home and a fortress in the Middle Ages.** It provided shelter for a king or a lord and his family, and it allowed him to defend his lands. Castles were also places where soldiers were stationed, wrong-doers were imprisoned, courts settled disputes, weapons and armour were made and great banquets and tournaments were held.

In the beginning

302 **The first castles were mostly built from wood on top of a hill.** Sometimes castle builders piled up soil to make the hill artificially. On top of the hill, called a motte, stood a wooden tower, or keep. This was the central part of the castle and the easiest part to defend.

▼ This is a motte and bailey castle. The Normans from France introduced this kind of castle in the 1000s, and it soon became popular across Europe.

◄ Castles and forts have been built all over the world since the earliest times. This is the fortified town of Great Zimbabwe, in modern day Zimbabwe. The oldest part dates from the 700s.

► By the 1500s the Japanese were building strong, permanent castles of their own. Castles were often built with different layers to fire on the enemy from different heights.

303 At the bottom of the motte was a courtyard called a bailey. It was usually surrounded by a wooden fence. Castle builders dug a deep ditch, called a moat, all around the outside of the motte and bailey. They often filled the moat with water. Moats were designed to stop attackers reaching the castle walls.

I DON'T BELIEVE IT!

The builders of the early wooden castles covered the walls with wet leather – to stop them from burning down.

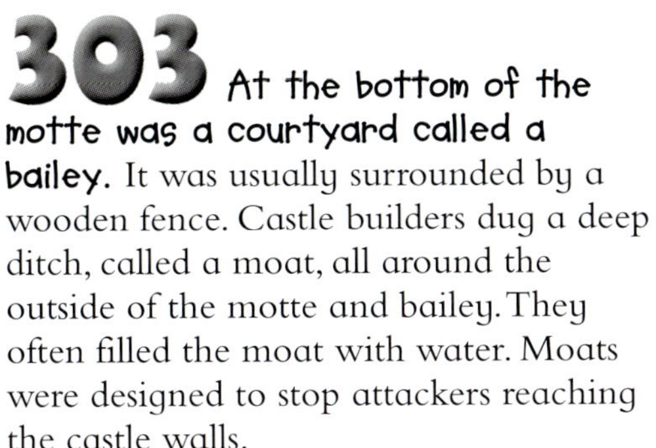

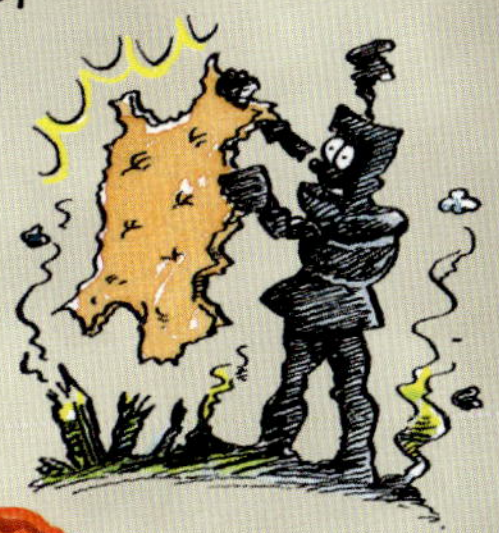

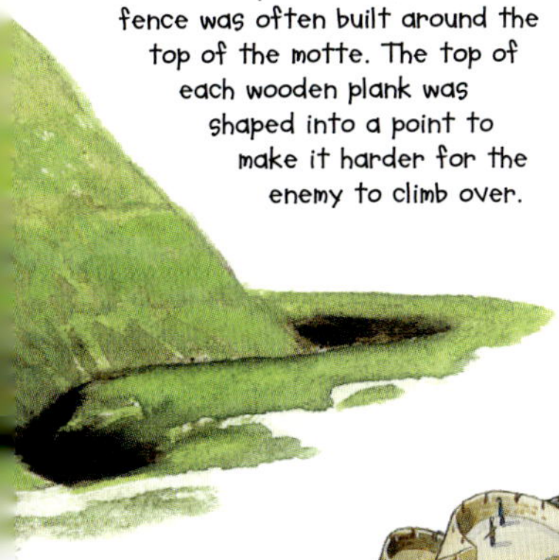

◀ For extra protection, a wooden fence was often built around the top of the motte. The top of each wooden plank was shaped into a point to make it harder for the enemy to climb over.

304 Wooden castles were not very strong – and they caught fire easily. From around 1100 onwards, people began to build castles in stone. A stone castle gave better protection against attack, fire and cold rainy weather.

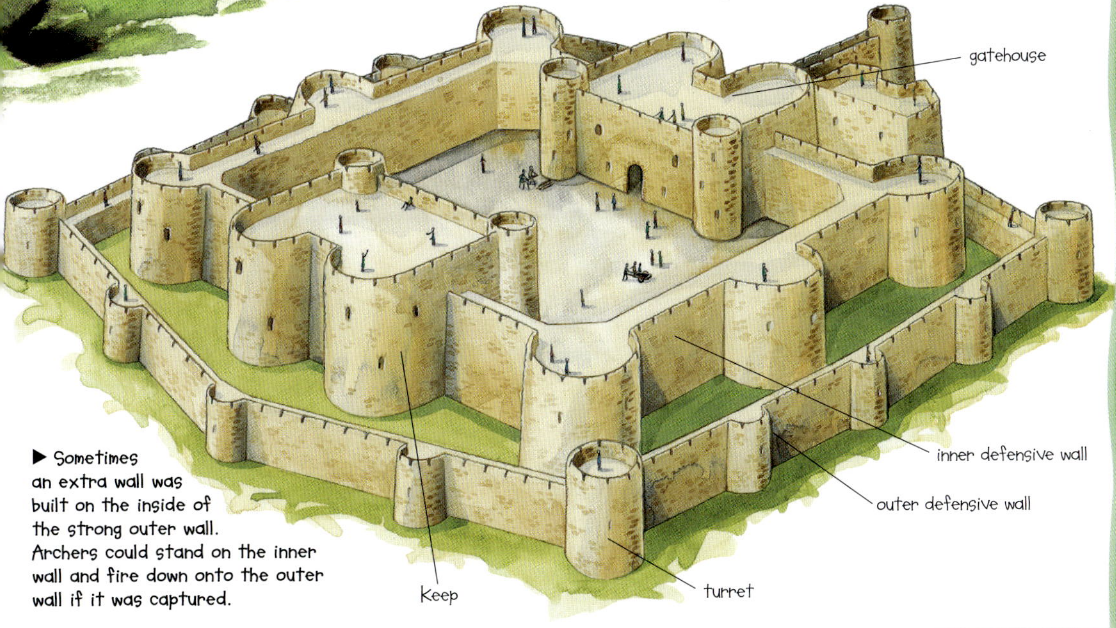

▶ Sometimes an extra wall was built on the inside of the strong outer wall. Archers could stand on the inner wall and fire down onto the outer wall if it was captured.

Building a castle

305 The best place to build a castle was on top of a hill. A hilltop position gave good views over the surrounding countryside, and made it harder for an enemy to launch a surprise attack. Sometimes a castle was built on the banks of a river or lake, and its waters were used to create a moat.

306

The lord of the castle and his family lived in the safest part of the castle — the keep. The walls of the keep were built to be very strong, and at least 3.5 metres thick in some castles. Inside the keep were large rooms for receiving visitors and holding banquets, as well as smaller storerooms and guardrooms. The family's bedrooms were on the top floor of the keep. All these rooms and defences made building a castle very slow and expensive.

DESIGN YOUR OWN CASTLE

Imagine you have been asked to design a castle for your local lord. It is important that he can defend his castle and his family against attacks by his enemies.

Draw a plan of your ideal castle, making sure it has plenty of defences. And don't forget the drawbridge to let the lord and his family in and out of their castle.

Who's who in the castle

307 A castle was the home of an important and powerful person, such as a king, a lord or a knight. The lord of the castle controlled the castle itself, as well as the lands and people around it. The lady of the castle was in charge of the day-to-day running of the castle. She controlled the kitchens and gave the servants their orders for feasts and banquets.

▶ Lord and lady of the manor

308 The constable was in charge of defending the castle. He was usually a fierce and ruthless man. He trained his soldiers to guard the castle properly and organized the rota of guards and watchmen. The constable was in charge of the whole castle when the lord was away.

309 Many servants lived and worked inside the castle, looking after the lord and his family. They cooked, cleaned, served at table, worked as maids and servants and ran errands. A man called the steward was in charge of all the servants.

310

Inside the castle walls were many workshops where goods were made and repaired. The castle blacksmith was kept busy making shoes for all the horses. The armourer made weapons and armour.

► The master of the horse had to look after the lord's horses.

311

Local villagers would shelter in the castle when their lands were under attack. They were not allowed to shelter inside the keep itself, so they stayed inside the bailey with their families and all their animals.

From kings to peasants

312 In medieval times, the king or queen was the most important person in the country. The king gave land to his barons and other noblemen. In return, they supplied the king with soldiers, horses and weapons to fight wars. This system of giving away land in return for services was known as feudalism.

▶ This bishop is having a meeting, called an audience, with the king and queen. In medieval times there was often conflict between the Church and the king. Both were very powerful, and they had to try to work together.

313 The Church was very powerful in the Middle Ages. It controlled large areas of land, and grew rich from the taxes paid by the peasants who worked on these lands. Peasant farmers had to give the church a tithe, one-tenth of everything they produced.

314

The barons were the most powerful noblemen. A wealthy baron might supply the king with around 5000 fighting men. Some barons also had their own private army to keep control over their own lands.

315

The wealthier lords and barons often gave away some of their lands to professional fighters called knights. Knights were skilled soldiers who rode into battle on horseback.

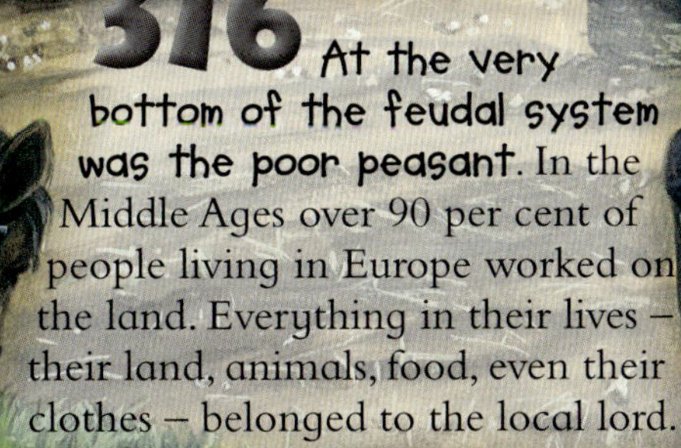

316

At the very bottom of the feudal system was the poor peasant. In the Middle Ages over 90 per cent of people living in Europe worked on the land. Everything in their lives — their land, animals, food, even their clothes — belonged to the local lord.

Quiz

1. What is the name of the mound of soil on which early castles were built?
2. Which was the safest and best-protected part of the castle?
3. What is a moat?
4. Who was in charge of the castle guards?
5. What did the king give to his lords in return for their services?

ANSWERS:
1. a motte 2. the keep 3. a water-filled ditch around the outside of the castle walls 4. the constable 5. land

How to be a good knight

317 **It took about 14 years of training to become a knight.** The son of a noble joined a lord's household aged seven. He learned how to ride, to shoot a bow and arrow and how to behave in front of nobles. He then became a squire, where he learned how to fight with a sword, and he looked after his master's armour and weapons. If he was successful, he became a knight at 21.

318 **The ceremony of making a new knight was known as dubbing.** A knight had to spend a whole night in church before his dubbing ceremony took place. This all-night watch was called a vigil. First, he had a cold bath and dressed in a plain white tunic. Then he spent the night on his knees in church, praying and confessing his sins.

319
The dubbing ceremony changed over time. In the beginning a knight was struck on the back of the neck. Later, dubbing involved a tap on the knight's shoulder with a sword.

A French knight called Jaufré Rudel sent love poems to the Countess of Tripoli even though he had never met her. When he finally saw her beautiful face he fell into her arms and died.

320
Knights had to behave according to a set of rules, known as the 'code of chivalry'. The code involved being brave and honourable on the battlefield, and treating the enemy politely and fairly. It also instructed knights how to behave towards women.

321
A knight who behaved badly was disgraced and punished. A knight in disgrace had either behaved in a cowardly way on the battlefield, cheated in a tournament or treated another knight badly.

322
A rich knight would have three horses. He rode his heaviest horse for fighting and tournaments. He also had a horse for riding, and a baggage horse. The best horses were warhorses from Italy and Spain. They were quick but strong and sturdy.

Ready for battle

323 Knights wore a long-sleeved tunic made of linen or wool, with a cloak over the top. By the 1200s knights had started to wear long hooded coats called surcoats. Knights nearly always wore bright colours, and some even wore fancy items such as shoes with curled pointed toes, and hats decorated with sparkling jewels.

◀ A knight was dressed for battle from the feet upwards. The last item of armour to be put on him was his helmet.

324 Early knights wore a type of armour called chainmail. It was made of thousands of tiny iron rings joined onto each other. A piece of chainmail looked a bit like knitting, except it was made of metal, not wool. But a knight also wore a padded jacket under his chainmail to make sure he wasn't cut by his own armour!

325 Gradually, knights began to wear more and more armour. They added solid metal plates shaped to fit their body. By the 1400s knights were wearing full suits of steel armour. They wore metal gloves, called gauntlets, and even metal shoes!

326 A knight had two main weapons: his sword and his shield. The sword was double edged and was sharp enough to pierce chainmail. Knights also fought with lances, daggers and axes.

◀ These knights are fighting in battle. The knight on the right has the usual weapons of a sword and shield. The knight on the left has a morning star. This was a spiked ball on the end of a chain.

327 Between 1337 and 1453 England and France were almost continually at war with each other, what we now know as the Hundred Years' War. The English armies won important battles against the French in 1356 and at Agincourt in 1415. The skilled English and Welsh longbowmen, who could fire as many as 12 arrows every minute, helped to stop the French knights.

328 A Swiss foot soldier's main weapon was a halberd. This was a combined spear and battleaxe, and was a particularly nasty, but very effective, way of a foot soldier getting a knight off his horse.

Colours and coats of arms

329 When a knight went into battle in full armour wearing a helmet with a visor, no one could recognize him. This problem was solved by putting a different set of coloured symbols on each knight's shield. These sets of symbols became known as coats of arms, and each family had its own personal design. No other family was allowed to use that design.

◀ Heraldry, the system of using coats of arms, became a very complex system of signs and symbols. Schools of heraldry were set up to sort out disputes over coats of arms.

330 Only certain colours and styles of design could be used to create a coat of arms. The colours allowed were red, blue, black, green, purple, silver and gold. The arms also indicated the wearer's position in his family. So, a second son showed a crescent symbol, and a seventh son displayed a rose.

331 On the battlefield, each nobleman had his own banner around which his knights and other soldiers could meet. The nobleman's colours and coat of arms were displayed on the banner. Banners decorated with coats of arms also made a colourful display at tournaments and parades.

◄ The banner of a nobleman was a very important symbol during battle. If the person holding the banner was killed in battle, someone had to pick the banner up and raise it straight away.

332 Messengers called heralds carried messages between knights during battle. They had to be able to recognize each individual knight quickly. After coats of arms were introduced, the heralds became experts at identifying them. The system of using coats of arms became known as heraldry.

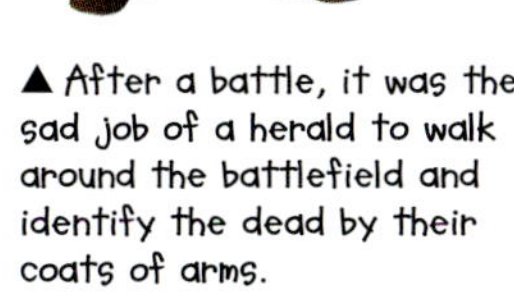

▲ After a battle, it was the sad job of a herald to walk around the battlefield and identify the dead by their coats of arms.

DESIGN YOUR OWN COAT OF ARMS

Would you like your own personal coat of arms? You can design one by following the basic rules of heraldry explained on these pages. You will need the seven paint colours listed opposite, a paintbrush, a fine-tipped black felt pen, a ruler and some thick white paper. Good luck!

Famous knights

333 Roland was a brave, loyal knight who died in the service of his master. Roland served King Charles the Great – Charlemagne – who ruled much of France and Germany in the 800s. Roland had to protect Charlemagne and his army from Muslim attackers as they crossed from Spain into France. But Roland was betrayed and died fighting for his king.

▲ Famous stories of old knights have been recorded in old books, like this one bound in leather.

334 The Spanish knight Rodrigo Díaz de Vivar had the nickname 'El Cid'. This comes from the Arabic for 'the Lord'. El Cid fought against the Moors from North Africa. He was exiled by his lord, King Alfonso VI, after the knight's enemies turned the king against him.

▼ Don Quixote charged at windmills because he thought they were giants.

▲ Rodrigo Díaz de Vivar, 'El Cid'.

335 The book 'Don Quixote' tells the story of an old man who dreams about past deeds of bravery and chivalry. It was written in the 1500s by a Spaniard called Miguel de Cervantes. After reading about the knights of old, Don Quixote dresses in armour and sets off on horseback to become famous. He takes a peasant called Sancho Panzo with him as his squire, and it is his squire who gets Don Quixote out of trouble during his travels.

336 Lancelot was the favourite knight of King Arthur. Tales of Arthur and his Knights of the Round Table were very popular in the 1200s. Lancelot fell in love with Arthur's wife Guinevere. The struggle between the two men, and the scandal caused by the romance between Lancelot and Guinevere, eventually destroyed Arthur's court.

337 The Black Prince was the nickname of Edward, the oldest son of Edward III of England. The Black Prince was a great warrior who captured the French king, John II, at the battle of Poitiers in 1356.

I DON'T BELIEVE IT!

During his travels Don Quixote mistakes flocks of farmyard animals for enemy armies!

A castle tour

338 Stone castles were cold damp places with lots of draughts. A castle was not exactly a luxury home. Cold winds blew through the windows, which had no glass.

▶ The lord of the castle and his family were the only people who slept in beds. Most people slept on wooden pallets covered with straw.

▶ Almost all castles also had a well within their walls. This was essential as a source of water if someone laid siege to the castle.

▶ The kitchens were often built in a separate part of the castle, away from the keep, in case they caught fire.

Quiz

1. Which were the two main battle weapons of a knight?

2. Why did knights start to display a coat of arms?

3. Who was Sir Lancelot?

4. Who was the Black Prince?

5. What was the name of the castle toilet?

ANSWERS:
1. A sword and a shield 2. To be recognized on the battlefield 3. The favourite knight of King Arthur 4. Prince Edward, the son of Edward III 5. The garderobe

▼ Castles had no central heating and no running water. Wool hangings and tapestries on the walls, and rugs on the floor, helped to warm the rooms. Roaring fires burned in the huge fireplaces.

339 There were many workshops and other buildings inside the safety of the castle walls. They included an armoury, a smithy, stables, kennels, a mill for making flour and a chapel. There were sometimes even gardens and orchards!

340 Medieval castles had no toilets! Instead people sat on wooden seats called 'garderobes'. These were built over a very long chute. Waste from the toilet fell down the chute into the moat.

◀ Every castle had a cold, dark and often slimy dungeon for keeping prisoners. The dungeon was usually located beneath one of the gatehouse towers. Prisoners would be locked inside a small airless cell.

Feasts and fun

341 **The Great Hall was the centre of castle life.** The lord and his family ate their meals here and carried out their daily business. Colourful banners and coats of arms and shiny pieces of armour hung from the walls of the Great Hall. The hall was sometimes turned into a courtroom to try local law-breakers.

342 **Musicians entertained the lord and his guests at banquets in the Great Hall.** They played instruments such as pipes, drums, fiddles and lutes.

343 **Jesters, jugglers and acrobats performed for the diners between courses.** Sometimes a dancing bear might be brought in to entertain the guests.

344

Huge amounts of exotic-looking and delicious foods were served at banquets.
Roast meats included stuffed peacock and swan, as well as venison, beef, goose, duck and wild boar. Whole roasted fish were also served.
These foods were followed by dishes made from spices brought from Asia, and then fruit and nuts.

BAKE A 'TARTE OF APPLES AND ORANGES'

You will need:

a packet of shortcrust pastry
4 eating apples
4 oranges
juice of $\frac{1}{2}$ lemon
3 cups of water
1 cup of honey

$\frac{1}{2}$ cup of brown sugar
$\frac{1}{4}$ tsp cinnamon
a pinch of dried ginger
a little milk
a little caster sugar

Ask an adult to help you. Line a pie dish with pastry and bake for 10 minutes in a medium-hot oven. Slice the oranges thinly. Boil the water, honey and lemon juice, add the oranges. Cover and simmer for 2 hours, then drain. Peel, core and slice the apples and mix with the sugar, cinnamon and ginger. Place a layer of apples in the bottom of the dish followed by a layer of oranges, then alternate layers until the fruit is used up. Place a pastry lid over the top and brush with a little milk. Make small slits in the lid. Bake in a medium-hot oven for about 45 minutes.

345

The lord, his family and important guests sat at the high table on a platform called a dais.
From their raised position they could look down over the rest of the diners. The most important guests such as priests and noblemen sat next to the lord.

346

Important guests drank fine wine out of proper glasses.
Cup-bearers poured the wine out of decorated pottery jugs. Less important diners drank ale or wine from mugs or tankards made of wood, pewter or leather.

Songs, poems and love

347 Medieval minstrels sang songs and recited poetry about love and bravery. These songs and poems showed knights as faithful, loving and religious men who were prepared to die for their king or lord. A true knight fought for justice and fairness for everyone. In real life, knights did not always live up to this ideal picture.

◀ Minstrels sang their songs to the accompaniment of sweet-sounding music from a harp or lute.

▼ Knights offered to perform brave and heroic acts at tournaments to prove the strength of their love.

348 A style of romantic behaviour called courtly love was popular among knights in both France and England. It was a kind of false love carried out by following strict rules. Courtly love stated that a knight had to fall in love with a woman of equal or higher rank – and ideally she should be married to someone else. Their love had to be kept secret.

349

Troubadours were poet-musicians who composed songs about heroic knights and ideal love. They lived in France in the 1100s and 1200s. Some troubadours had themselves been knights at one time, and they told rather exaggerated stories of their own deeds of love and bravery.

▲ Richard I of England, who is better known as Richard the Lionheart, was a troubadour. Some of the songs he wrote have been preserved.

350

A knight wrote secret letters to the woman he loved. He had to worship his loved one from a distance, and could never declare his love for a lady directly to her.

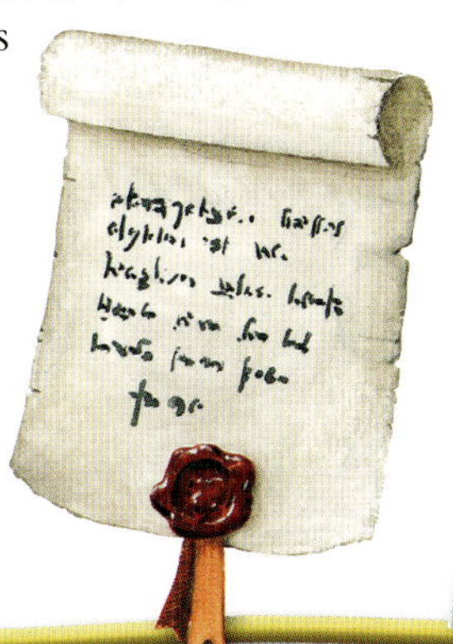

▶ A knight and his love wrote poems to each other, expressing their feelings of love and devotion.

ILLUMINATED LETTERS

The first letter of a manuscript, called an illuminated letter, was much larger than the others, and it was decorated with pictures and patterns.

You can create your own set of illuminated letters for the initials of your name. Draw the outline of the letter in fine black pen and then use felt-tipped pens or paints to add the decoration.

▶ An illuminated letter 'C'.

Knights and dragons

351 The legend of St George tells how the brave knight killed a fierce dragon. The dragon was terrorizing the people of Lydia (part of modern Turkey). The king offered his daughter to the dragon if the dragon left his people alone. St George arrived and said he would kill their dragon if they became Christians like him. Thousands accepted his offer, and George killed the dragon.

▲ St George was adopted as the patron saint of England in the 1300s.

352 Ivanhoe was a medieval knight who lived in the time of Richard the Lionheart. He is the hero of a historical book called 'Ivanhoe', written by the Scottish novelist Sir Walter Scott in the 1800s. 'Ivanhoe' describes the conflict between the Saxon people and their Norman conquerors at a time when the Normans had ruled England for at least 100 years.

353 Legend says that King Arthur became king after pulling a magic sword called Excalibur out of a stone. This act proved that he was the right person to rule Britain. People have written stories about Arthur and his followers, the Knights of the Round Table, for more than 1000 years.

◀ No one really knows who the real Arthur was, but he may have been a Celtic warrior who lived about 1400 years ago.

355 In the 1300s an Englishman called Geoffrey Chaucer wrote 'The Canterbury Tales'. These stories were about a group of pilgrims travelling from a London inn to a religious site in Canterbury. The pilgrims included a priest, a nun, a merchant, a cook, a ploughman and a knight and his squire.

354 King Arthur had many castle homes but his favourite was Camelot. Historians think that Camelot was really an English castle called Tintagel. When Arthur heard that his best friend and favourite knight, Sir Lancelot, had fallen in love with Arthur's wife, Queen Guinevere, Arthur banished Lancelot from his court at Camelot.

Quiz

1. What is a minstrel?
2. Whose job was it to fill everyone's glass at a banquet?
3. What did a troubadour do?
4. Who were the Knights of the Round Table?
5. What is the name of King Arthur's favourite castle?

ANSWERS:
1. A wandering musician
2. The cup-bearer 3. Write songs about knights and courtly love
4. The followers of King Arthur
5. Camelot

Practice for battle

356 In a tournament, knights divided into two sides and fought each other as if in a proper battle. Tournaments were good practice for the real thing – war. The idea for these mock battles, called tourneys, probably started in France in the 12th century.

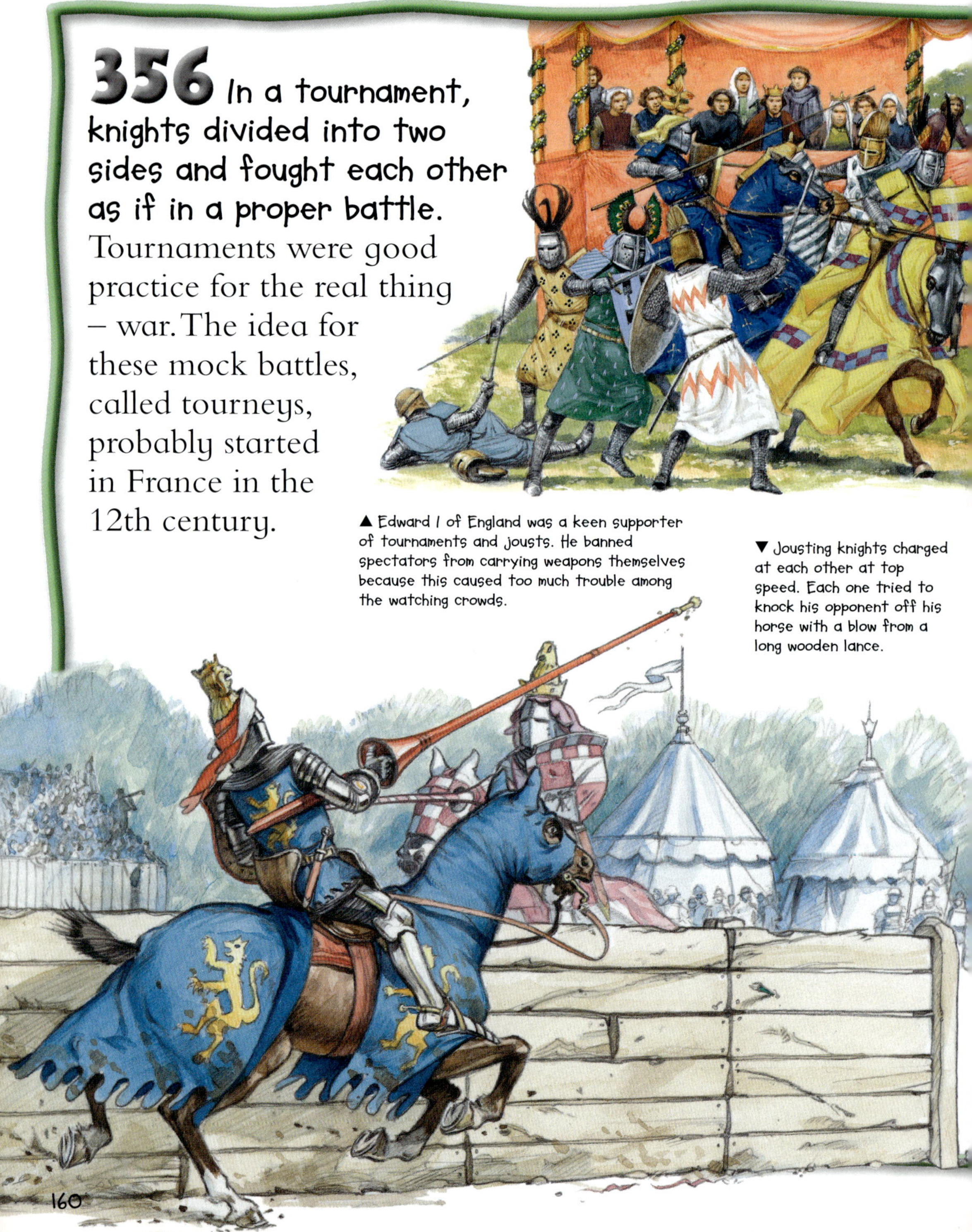

▲ Edward I of England was a keen supporter of tournaments and jousts. He banned spectators from carrying weapons themselves because this caused too much trouble among the watching crowds.

▼ Jousting knights charged at each other at top speed. Each one tried to knock his opponent off his horse with a blow from a long wooden lance.

357

Tournaments took place under strict rules. There were safe areas where knights could rest without being attacked by the other side. Knights were not meant to kill their opponents but they often did. Several kings became so angry at losing their best knights that all tournaments were banned unless the king had given his permission.

358

Jousting was introduced because so many knights were being killed or wounded during tournaments. More than 60 knights were killed in a single tourney in Cologne, Germany. Jousting was a fight between two knights on horseback. Each knight tried to win by knocking the other off his horse. Knights were protected by armour, and their lances were not sharp.

359

A knight's code of chivalry did not allow him to win a tournament by cheating. It was better to lose with honour than to win in disgrace.

I DON'T BELIEVE IT!

Some knights cheated in jousts by wearing special armour that was fixed onto the horse's saddle!

360

Sometimes the knights carried on fighting on the ground with their swords. The problem was that this was as dangerous as a tourney!

361

A joust gave a knight the chance to prove himself in front of the woman he loved. Jousts were very social events watched by ladies of the court as well as ordinary people. Knights could show off their skills and bravery to impress the spectators.

Friend or enemy?

362 When Edward the Confessor died in 1066, Duke William of Normandy, his cousin, claimed that he had been promised the throne of England. William and his knights invaded England and defeated Harold, the English king, at the Battle of Hastings.

▲ The Bayeux Tapestry records the story of the Norman invasion of England. It shows William and his knights landing along the English coast, and also shows the moment when England's King Harold was killed at the Battle of Hastings.

▲ Here you can see the route that William the Conqueror took to London.

363 On and off between 1337 and 1453 the neighbouring countries of England and France were at war. The Hundred Years' War, as it was called, carried on through the reigns of five English kings and five French ones. The two countries fought each other to decide who should control France. In the end the French were victorious, and England lost control of all her lands in France apart from the port of Calais.

364 One of the major battles of the Hundred Years' War was fought at Crécy in 1346. English soldiers defeated a much larger French army, killing almost half the French soldiers. During the battle, the English army used gunpowder and cannons for possibly the first time.

365 Deadly weapons called caltrops were used in the Hundred Years' War. A caltrop was a star-shaped piece of metal. These were scattered along the ground in front of an attacking army. They stopped both horses and footsoldiers in their tracks.

366 A young French girl called Joan of Arc led the French army against the English, who had surrounded the city of Orléans. After 10 days the English were defeated. Joan was later captured, accused of being a witch, and burned to death.

Under attack

367 An attacking enemy had to break through a castle's defences to get inside its walls. One method was to break down the castle gates with giant battering rams. Attackers and defenders also used siege engines to hurl boulders at each other.

368 A siege is when an enemy surrounds a castle and stops all supplies from reaching the people inside. The idea is to starve the castle occupants until they surrender or die.

369 A riskier way of trying to get inside a castle was to climb over the walls. Attackers either used ladders or moved wooden towers with men hidden inside them into position beside the walls.

370

Giant catapults were sometimes uses to fire stones or burning pieces of wood inside the castle. The Romans were some of the first people to use catapults in warfare.

▶ Attackers could also dig a tunnel under a wall or a tower. They would then light a fire that burnt away the tunnel's supports. The tunnel collapsed, and brought down the building above.

▲ This siege engine was called a trebuchet. It had a long wooden arm with a heavy weight at one end and a sling at the other. A heavy stone was placed inside the sling. As the weight dropped, the stone was hurled towards the castle walls, sometimes travelling as far as 300 metres.

371

The enemy sometimes succeeded in tunnelling beneath the castle walls. They surprised the defenders when they appeared inside the castle itself.

▶ Cannons were first used to attack castles and fortified towns and cities in the 1300s. Early cannons, called bombards, were made of bronze or iron and they were not very accurate.

372

The invention of cannons and gunpowder brought the building of castle strongholds almost to an end. It marked the end of warrior knights too. Castle walls could not stand up to the powerful cannonballs that exploded against them. Guns and cannons were now used on the battlefield, so armies no longer needed the services of brave armoured knights on horseback.

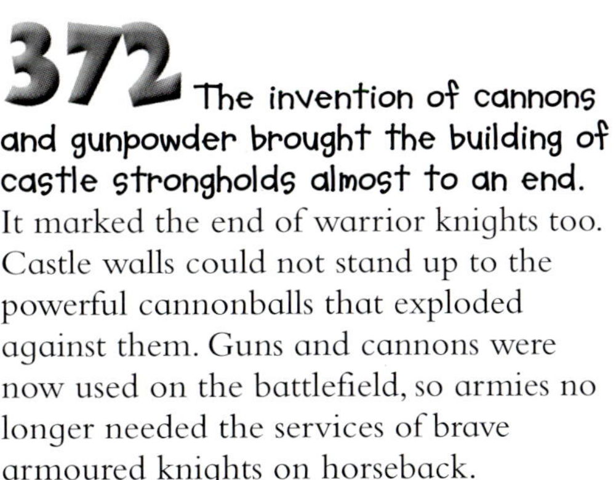

Defending a castle

373 When the enemy was first spotted approaching a castle, its defenders first pulled up the castle drawbridge. They also lowered an iron grate, called a portcullis, to form an extra barrier behind the drawbridge.

374 The castle archers fired their arrows through narrow slits in the thick castle walls. They also fired through the gaps in the battlements.

▶ Soldiers could use a longbow while the enemy was still a long way away.

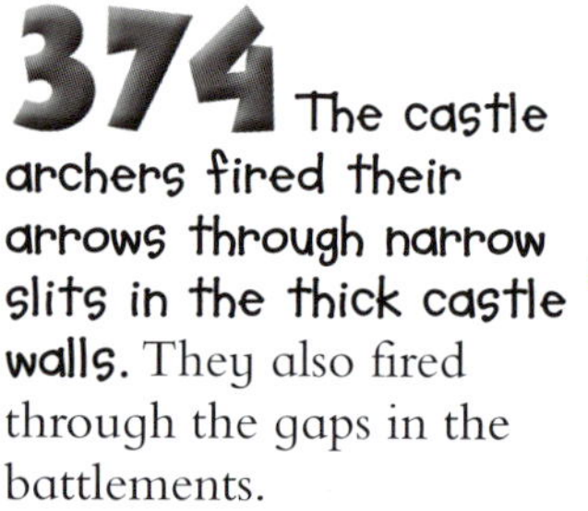

▶ Crossbows were far slower to aim and fire than longbows.

375 In the middle of the night, a raiding party might leave a besieged castle to surprise the enemy camped outside. The raiders would move along secret passages and climb out through hidden gates or doorways.

376 Defenders poured boiling–hot water onto the heads of the enemy as they tried to climb the castle walls. Quicklime was also poured over the enemy soldiers, making their skin burn.

▶ Water was poured onto the enemy's heads through holes in the stonework of the battlements.

377 Heavy stones and other missiles often rained down from the battlements onto the enemy below. Hidden from view by the high battlements, the defenders stood on wooden platforms to throw the missiles.

Off to the crusades

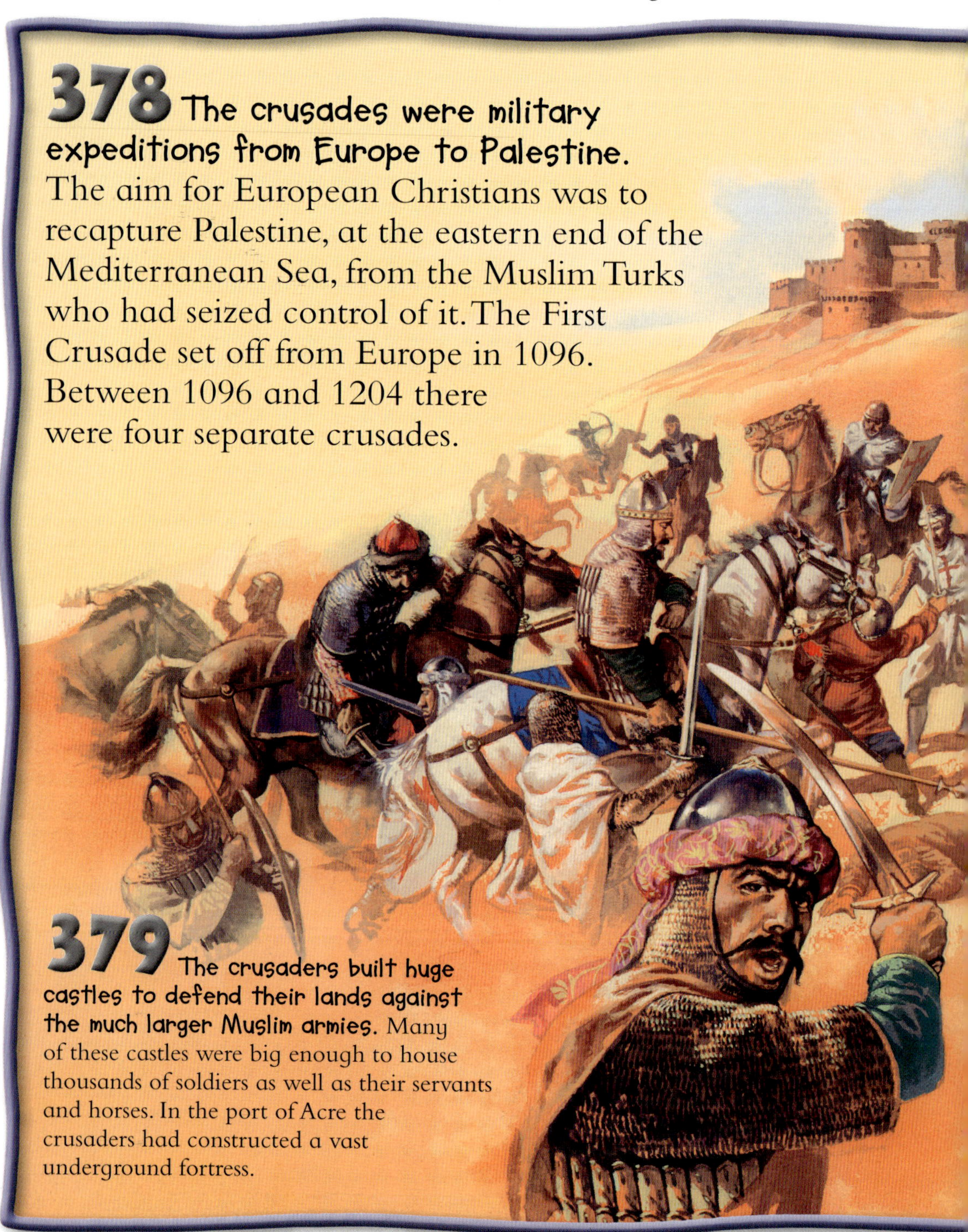

378 **The crusades were military expeditions from Europe to Palestine.** The aim for European Christians was to recapture Palestine, at the eastern end of the Mediterranean Sea, from the Muslim Turks who had seized control of it. The First Crusade set off from Europe in 1096. Between 1096 and 1204 there were four separate crusades.

379 **The crusaders built huge castles to defend their lands against the much larger Muslim armies.** Many of these castles were big enough to house thousands of soldiers as well as their servants and horses. In the port of Acre the crusaders had constructed a vast underground fortress.

380

Thousands of young boys and girls set off for the Holy Land in 1212 in one of the strangest crusades – the Children's Crusade. Many died of cold or hunger while marching to the Mediterranean ports. Others drowned during the sea crossing, and some were sold as slaves along the way.

381

The Muslim leader Saladin fought against the knights of the Third Crusade. Saladin had already defeated the Christian armies and seized the city of Jerusalem. The Third Crusade was meant to recapture Jerusalem. It was led by an emperor and two kings: Emperor Frederick I of Germany, and Richard the Lionheart of England and Philip II of France, but the crusaders failed to regain Jerusalem.

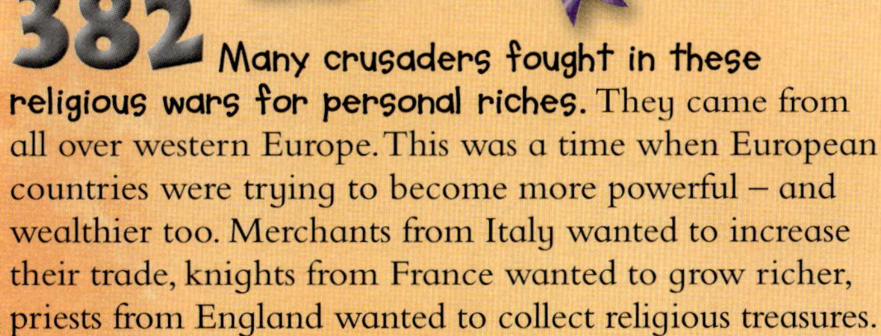

382

Many crusaders fought in these religious wars for personal riches. They came from all over western Europe. This was a time when European countries were trying to become more powerful – and wealthier too. Merchants from Italy wanted to increase their trade, knights from France wanted to grow richer, priests from England wanted to collect religious treasures.

Garters and elephants

383 A group of Christian knights living in the Holy Land were in charge of protecting pilgrims on their way to and from Palestine. They were the Templar knights, or Templars. Their headquarters were in the Aqsa Mosque in the city of Jerusalem. The Templars grew very rich during their time in the Holy Land, but their organization was eventually broken up.

384 The Knights of St John looked after the safety and health of pilgrims while they were in the Holy Land. The knights lived like monks and followed strict rules, but they also continued to provide soldiers to fight the Muslims.

▶ The Knights of St John had been monks who cared for sick people before becoming religious knights. They were often referred to as the Hospitallers.

385 Medieval knights began to band together to form special groups called orders. Each order had its own badge showing the symbol chosen by the order. It was considered an honour to be asked to join an order. New orders began to appear in many countries across Europe. The Order of the Golden Fleece, for example, was started in France by Philip the Good.

▲ Knights wore the badge of their order on a chain around the neck. Knights from the Order of the Golden Fleece wore a badge depicting a golden sheep.

386

The Order of the Bath was founded in Britain in the early 1400s. Knights who belonged to an order swore loyalty to their king or queen, and promised to fight against their enemies.

387

The Order of the Garter is the oldest and most important order in Britain. According to the story, Edward III was dancing with a countess when she lost her garter. As the king gave it back to her, he heard the people near him laughing and joking about what they had seen. Angry, the king said that anyone who had evil thoughts should be ashamed. This is still the motto of the order.

▼ The emblem of the Order of the Garter is a dark-blue garter trimmed with gold. Knights of the order wear it on their left leg at important ceremonies.

Quiz

1. Which Muslim warrior fought against the knights of the Third Crusade?
2. By what other name is Richard I of England known?
3. In which city can you find important Muslim and Christian sites?
4. What do knights of the Order of the Golden Fleece wear around their necks?

ANSWERS:
1. Saladin
2. Richard the Lionheart
3. Jerusalem 4. A golden sheep

388

The Order of the Elephant from Denmark is more than 500 years old. Members of the order wear a badge that features an elephant waving its trunk in the air.

Warriors from the East

389 Warrior knights in Japan in the Middle Ages were known as samurai. People in Japan were also divided into different feudal groups, where people in each group served someone in a higher-ranking group. The samurai, like European knights, served a lord. They usually fought on horseback but later on they began to fight more on foot.

▼ The Seljuk Turks were named after their first leader, Seljuk.

390 A long curving sword was a samurai warrior's most treasured possession. Samurai warriors wore armour on the bodies, arms and legs, a helmet and often a crest made up of a pair of horns.

391 The fierce Seljuk Turks fought against Christian knights during the crusades. The Seljuks swept across southwest Asia in the 1000s and 1100s. They conquered many lands, including Syria, Palestine, Asia Minor (modern Turkey) and Persia (modern Iran).

392

Fierce Mongol warriors from the East terrifed the enemy in battle. The Mongols were expert horsemen who controlled their horses with their feet while standing up in their stirrups. This way of riding left both hands free to shoot a bow and arrow.

▼ Each Mongol warrior had a team of five horses ready for battle. As well as being skilled archers, the Mongols were highly trained spear-throwers.

393

Genghis Khan was the greatest of the Mongol leaders. He became leader of his tribe when he was just 13 years old. He united all the Mongol tribes, and went on to conquer northern China, Korea, northern India, Afghanistan, Persia and parts of Russia.

I DON'T BELIEVE IT!

The Turks fought with gold pieces in their mouth – to stop the crusader knights from stealing their gold. If a Turkish warrior thought he was going to die, he swallowed the gold.

Famous castles

394 Many castles are said to be haunted by the ghosts of people who died within their walls. Many of these ghosts are kings and queens who were killed by their sworn enemies. Edward II of England was murdered in his cell at Berkeley Castle in southwest England. Richard II died at Pontefract Castle in Yorkshire.

▼ Visitors to Berkeley Castle say they can hear the screams of the murdered Edward at night.

Windsor Castle

395 English kings and queens have lived at Windsor Castle since William the Conqueror began building it more than 900 years ago. William's original castle consisted of a wooden fort on top of an earth motte, with earthworks around the bailey area. The first stone buildings were added in the 1100s.

396 Glamis Castle in Scotland is the scene for the play 'Macbeth' by William Shakespeare. In the play, the ambitious Macbeth plots with his evil wife to kill the Scottish king, Duncan, and claim the throne for himself. In real life, Macbeth did defeat and kill Duncan in 1040.

Glamis Castle

Bodiam Castle

397 The moated Bodiam Castle in southern England was built in the 1300s to keep out attacking French armies. An English knight, Sir Edward Dalyngrigge, believed that the French were about to invade his lands. His castle home had a curtain wall broken up by round towers.

▼ The castle at Krak des Chevaliers that visitors see today is almost unchanged from the 1300s and 1400s. This remarkable castle was the home of the Hospitaller knights.

398 The huge crusader castle of Krak des Chevaliers in Syria is perched on a hill of solid rock with far-reaching views over the surrounding countryside. A ditch between the castle's massive outside wall, with its 13 towers, and the inside wall was filled with water from a nearby aqueduct. This moat was used to supply the castle baths and to water the knights' horses.

399 The town of Carcassonne in southern France is rather like one huge castle. The whole town is surrounded by high walls and towers that were built in the Middle Ages.

400 The hilltop castle of Neuschwanstein was built long after the Middle Ages – work on the castle started in 1869. The fairytale castle was the dream project of 'mad' King Ludwig of Bavaria. The government of Bavaria removed the king from power because his ambitious castle-building plans cost too much money.

◄ Today, Neuschwanstein Castle is one of Germany's most popular tourist attractions. The castle was the model for the Magic Kingdom castle in Walt Disney's theme park in California, USA.

401 **Special forces are small groups of carefully selected soldiers.** They are highly trained and their task is to go on secret and dangerous missions. For example, they could be ordered to make a daring attack on a target deep inside enemy territory (land). Today they play a vital role in the fight against terrorism.

▲ There's often no time on a special forces mission to stop in a nice, dry place. Here, Russian Spetsnaz soldiers jump from their moving Armoured Personal Carrier straight into the water, with guns at the ready.

BANDS OF HEROES

◀ This 5th to 6th century BC frieze in the palace of the Persian King Darius at Susa shows the Immortals.

402 **The Immortals were the elite troops of the Persian Empire in the 6th century BC.** They were called Immortals because it was thought that there were always exactly 10,000 of them. Any soldier who was killed or badly wounded was at once replaced by a highly trained reserve. Immortals carried spears with silver handles and wore coats made of metal scales beneath their robes.

403 **The Spartans were a warrior people who fought in ancient Greece.** Spartan soldiers were renowned for their toughness and lived on only the bare necessities. Today the word 'spartan' means stern, disciplined and without luxury.

404 **A band of just 300 Spartan soldiers, led by King Leonidas, fought a heroic last stand at the Battle of Thermopylae in 480 BC.** Thermopylae was a narrow pass and its name means 'hot gates'. With just a few hundred others, the Spartans held the pass for seven days against a Persian army that may have numbered more than 100,000. However they were all killed, eventually.

▼ An artist's impression of how the Spartans might have looked as they braced themselves for their heroic stand against the might of Persia at Thermopylae in 480 BC.

◄ The highest officials in the Roman Empire were always protected by the tough soldiers of the Praetorian Guard, shown here wearing blue and orange.

405

The Praetorian Guard were the Roman emperor's personal bodyguard. They were set up by Emperor Augustus in 31 BC to protect him from being murdered, as his father Julius Caesar was. Their symbol was a scorpion. The Guard became more and more powerful and ruthless. In the end, they actually assassinated emperors if they did not approve of them, rather than protecting them. So for centuries, the Guard decided who became emperor.

◄ In 11th century Byzantium, no one messed with the fierce Viking soldiers of the Varangian Guard, who fought with huge axes.

► Varangian sword, 9th century Russia

406

The Varangian Guard were Viking warriors who protected an emperor. Byzantium was a vast empire centred on modern Istanbul that lasted for 1100 years, from the 4th to the 15th century. In the 11th century, the Emperor Basil brought in rough, tough Viking warriors from Russia to be his guard. They fought only with axes and were loyal to no one but each other. The most famous of them was Harald Hardrada, who died trying to conquer England in 1066.

SWORDS AND HORSES

407 **The Knights Templar were an order (group) of Christian knights that is now surrounded by legend.** They were set up by nine knights in 1119 to protect pilgrims visiting the Holy Land (Palestine), and named for their base at Temple Mount in Jerusalem. The Templars became wealthy and powerful, but caused resentment among rival orders. On Friday 13 October, 1307, the order was disbanded by the Pope.

► Templar knights were famous for their courage and skill with swords.

408 **Ninja were Japanese warriors with amazing skills who fought with katana (curved swords).** Often pictured in black tunics and masks, they usually travelled in disguise. Their task was to sneak into enemy territory to identify weak defences, set fire to enemy castles and assassinate enemy leaders. Ninja equipment included special ropes and hooks for scaling castle walls.

▲ Ninjas could climb so swiftly and silently that people said they must be able to fly into enemy castles.

409 **The Ninja were so secretive and skilled that people thought they must be magical.** Some stories say that they could cause enemies to become rooted to the spot with a touch of their hand. It was also believed that they could fly on kites, become invisible and change into animals.

► Few soldiers have ever been more glamorous than the Korean flower knights who went into battle wearing make-up and beautiful silk robes.

410 **The Hwarang were the flower knights of 8th century Silla in Korea.** They were probably called 'flower knights' because they were young noblemen who wore make-up and very flowery robes. Famed for their extraordinary skill with swords and for never retreating in battle, the Hwarang were also inspired by the spiritual teachers Confucius and Buddha. The most famous Hwarang was Kim Yu-Shin, who unified Korea in the 8th century.

411 **Cossacks were warriors from southern Ukraine and Russia, known for their courage and horsemanship.** Boys born into Cossack communities were rocked to sleep with war songs rather than lullabies, and taught to ride as soon as they could walk. They boasted that 100 Cossack horsemen were quieter than a single ordinary soldier. In the 18th century they became the Russian emperor's 'eyes', looking out for signs of trouble.

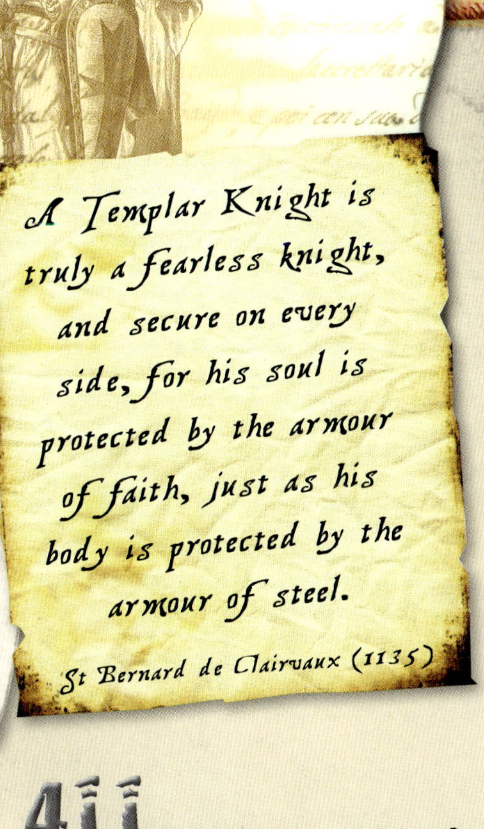

◄ The Cossacks of Russia were famed for their supreme horsemanship and their toughness – and also for their wild parties.

SCOUTS AND RAIDERS

412 **American Indian dog soldiers made sure they fought to the last.** Every year, four soldiers were chosen to wear a length of leather called the dog-rope. During battle each soldier attached the free end of his rope to the ground, pinning himself to the spot, and would not free himself until his comrades were safe. The dog soldiers led the last fight of the Cheyenne people against the American settlers in the mid–1800s.

▶ Dog soldiers wore huge, distinctive headdresses, which they made by sticking bird feathers into their caps.

413 **For the US cavalry, American Indian scouts were the unsung heroes of the Indian Wars in the 19th century.** These were a series of conflicts between the US government and the American Indians. In 1860 the president authorized the US cavalry to take on 1000 American Indians as scouts (guides). The scouts' inside knowledge of the land and their targets made them a highly effective weapon for the cavalry.

▲ In their fight against the American Indians, the US cavalry relied on American Indian scouts such as these five Apaches, who were renowned for their uncanny tracking ability.

◄ The raids made by small bands of Confederates in the American Civil War inspired legends.

415 **The Lovat Scouts have been described as 'half-wolf, half-jackrabbit'.** They were formed in 1900 to carry out raids and observation for the British in the Boer War (1899–1902). Some learnt their skills as ghillies (hunting guides) in the Scottish mountains. They sometimes wore ghillie suits (body camouflage) and many were crack shots. The Lovat Scouts later became the first sniper units. Snipers are sharpshooters who fire on their targets from hidden positions.

414 **During the American Civil War (1861–1865), legends were inspired by raiding parties.** These were groups of men sent by the Confederate army to attack towns deep within the territory of the opposing Unionists. The most famous was Morgan's Raid in 1863, when the raiding party rode 1600 kilometres in 46 days. They did a great deal of damage, but few came back alive. One who did was 'Stovepipe' Johnson, who had led an earlier raid to capture the town of Newburgh, Indiana, in 1862.

► A pair of Lovat scouts, wearing their 'ghillie' camouflage suits, take part in a training exercise.

QUICK-FIRE QUIZ

1. How many dog soldiers wore the dog-rope each year?
2. What is a ghillie suit?
3. Who led the raid that captured the town of Newburgh in 1862?

Answers:
1. Four 2. A form of body camouflage 3. 'Stovepipe' Johnson

416

The US Army Corps of Signals was the first specialist communications force. The armies of World War I (1914–1918) had to keep in touch over vast distances and quickly pass on information about enemy activity. When the USA entered World War I (1917), the US Army Corps of Signals developed the first radiotelephones so commanders could talk directly by radio on the battlefield.

▲ US Army Signal Corps, shown here in 1918 with their field telephone. Its development enabled commanders to talk directly to each other on the battlefield for the first time.

▼ An aerial photo taken from an airship in May 1916 during World War I.

▶ During World War I, a co-pilot would lean out of the open cockpit of his scouting plane to drop bombs on enemy targets by hand.

417

Spying from the air was the task of reconnaissance units. During the French Revolutionary Wars (1792–1802), the French used hot-air balloons to spy on their enemies, but it was in World War I that aerial reconnaissance (observation from the air) really took off. Some missions were in planes, with a pilot and an observer. At first, the observers drew pictures but later cameras were used. In some cases, an observer had to dangle on a rope far below an airship hidden in the clouds!

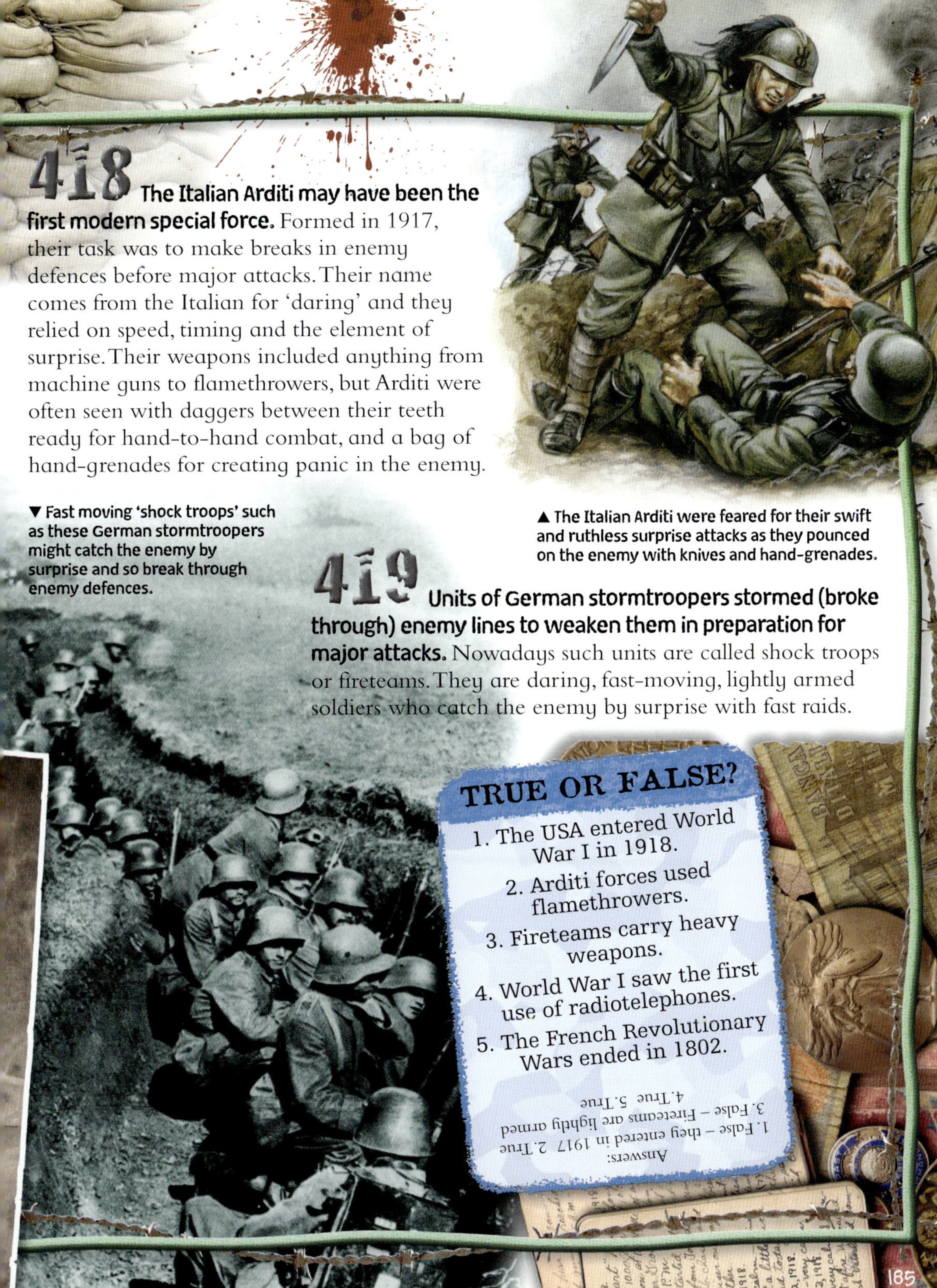

418 **The Italian Arditi may have been the first modern special force.** Formed in 1917, their task was to make breaks in enemy defences before major attacks. Their name comes from the Italian for 'daring' and they relied on speed, timing and the element of surprise. Their weapons included anything from machine guns to flamethrowers, but Arditi were often seen with daggers between their teeth ready for hand-to-hand combat, and a bag of hand-grenades for creating panic in the enemy.

▼ Fast moving 'shock troops' such as these German stormtroopers might catch the enemy by surprise and so break through enemy defences.

▲ The Italian Arditi were feared for their swift and ruthless surprise attacks as they pounced on the enemy with knives and hand-grenades.

419 **Units of German stormtroopers stormed (broke through) enemy lines to weaken them in preparation for major attacks.** Nowadays such units are called shock troops or fireteams. They are daring, fast-moving, lightly armed soldiers who catch the enemy by surprise with fast raids.

TRUE OR FALSE?

1. The USA entered World War I in 1918.
2. Arditi forces used flamethrowers.
3. Fireteams carry heavy weapons.
4. World War I saw the first use of radiotelephones.
5. The French Revolutionary Wars ended in 1802.

Answers:
1. False – they entered in 1917 2. True 3. False – Fireteams are lightly armed 4. True 5. True

WORLD WAR II

420 In World War II (1939–1945), British Prime Minister Winston Churchill created a force called the Commandos. They made daring raids from Britain in enemy-occupied Europe. In 1942 they attacked a dock at the French port of St Nazaire, vital to the Germans for repairing the battleship *Tirpitz*. The British sent a ship packed with explosives to ram the dock gates while the Commandos destroyed the dock facilities.

▲ British Commandos crawl forward under sniper fire during an attack in the last months of World War II. Commandos wore red berets to show enemy soldiers that they were part of an elite force.

▶ David Stirling (in the cap) with soldiers from the Long Range Desert Group that helped him try out ideas for the SAS in the North African desert in 1942.

421 The British Special Air Service (SAS) is the most famous special force. It was set up in North Africa in 1941 by David Stirling, who was nicknamed 'The Phantom Major' because he could slip like a ghost in and out of enemy territory. On their first mission, SAS forces used parachutes for a raid on German airfields in the Sahara, but bad weather blew them off course. After that most raids were high-speed dashes in armed jeeps. The SAS proved so effective that it is the inspiration for all special forces today.

422

With parachutes, special forces could be dropped quickly and quietly into enemy territory. US Airborne Divisions prepared the ground for the Allied invasion of Normandy, France, in 1944. On the night of 5–6 June, 1944, 13,100 soldiers were dropped inside German-occupied France, with orders to seize and hold vital enemy targets. Each man carried over 32 kilograms of equipment as well as his parachute. They succeeded in spreading confusion behind enemy lines, but many were killed.

423

The US 1st Special Service Force (SSF) was known by the Germans as the 'Black Devils'. They were famed for capturing 'impossible' targets – climbing cliffs in the dead of night, blackening their faces to make themselves less visible, and knocking out guards silently in hand-to-hand combat. They often caught their enemies so much off-guard that they were able to disarm them without a shot being fired. Wherever they went they left stickers saying *Das dicke Ende kommt noch*, which in German means, 'The worst is yet to come'.

424

Australian coastwatchers played a vital role in the Allied fight against the Japanese in the Pacific Ocean. Their job was to hide alone on Pacific islands, keeping a constant watch on the movements of Japanese forces. They often recruited native people to help, and rescued many troops captured by the Japanese.

▲ In World War II, special forces such as the Commandos became skilled in parachuting behind enemy lines under cover of darkness. It was very dangerous, but helped them catch the enemy by surprise.

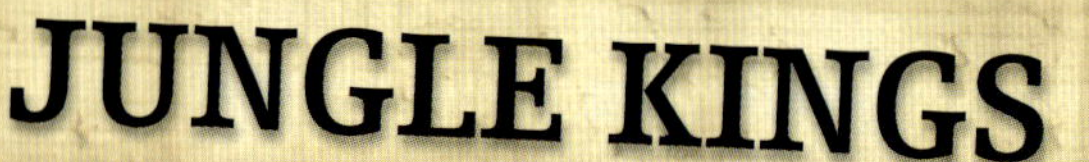

JUNGLE KINGS

425 **'Better to die than be a coward' is the motto of the Gurkha soldiers of Nepal.** They first fought for the British as long ago as 1815, but they became famous in World War II for their skill and bravery in jungle warfare.

▼ The Royal Gurkha rifles, seen here training at The Royal Military Academy Sandhurst in England, are regarded as some of the world's best soldiers.

▲ The sharp, curved blade of the kukri looks lethal but Gurkhas insist it is used mainly for cooking!

426 **A Gurkha always carries a long, curved blade called a kukri.** It was said that once a kukri was drawn, it had to taste enemy blood – or the owner would have to cut himself.

▼ This map shows the route taken by the Chindits on their epic raid through Japanese lines in the Burmese jungle in Operation Longcloth.

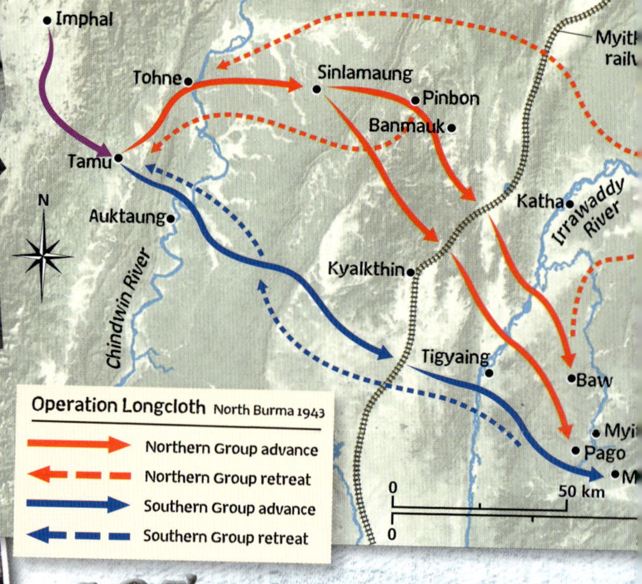

Gurkhas from the British Army on parade in India.

427 **The Chindits were Britain's biggest special force in World War II.** They were specialists in jungle warfare against the Japanese in Burma. In Operation Longcloth in 1943, they marched more than 1500 kilometres in humid and difficult terrain, far into enemy territory.

428

The US 'Merrill's Marauders' earned their nickname by undertaking an astonishing raid in 1944. Their commander, Brigadier General Frank Merrill, led his men right through Burma to the northern town of Myitkyina to cut a vital railway line and to perform acts of sabotage behind Japanese lines.

▶ Helicopters have become crucial for special forces operating in jungle territory. They can drop a small raiding force deep in the jungle – or pick it up again like this if the going gets tough.

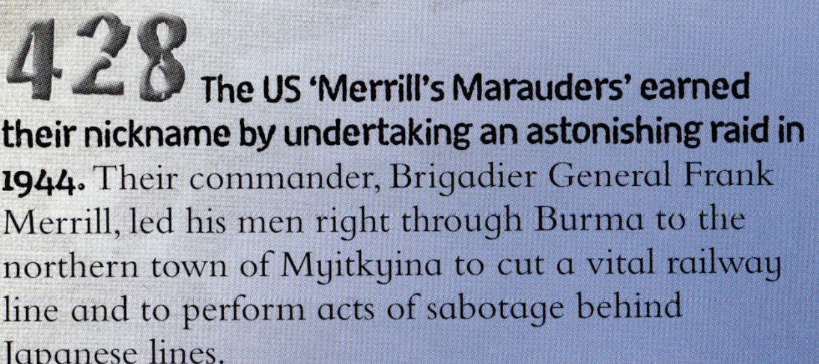

▲ Using only light gear that could be carried on their backs or on mules, Merrill's Marauders used the cover of the Burmese jungle to make daring raids.

429

The Malayan Scouts had incredible survival techniques. It was said that no army patrol could endure jungle terrain for much more than a week, but the Scouts were able to last for months. It is impossible to parachute into thick jungle, so the Scouts pioneered the technique of climbing down ropes into treetops from helicopters.

BRITISH SPECIAL FORCES

430 **Britain's special forces come under the umbrella 'UKSF' – United Kingdom Special Forces.** They include specialist SAS units trained for reconnaissance and to fight terrorism, and SBS (Special Boat Service) units, which focus on terrorism at sea, and special missions on coasts and in swamps.

▶ The SAS's badge shows a flaming sword in a crusader shield. It was inspired by the British victory at Tobruk in Operation Crusader in World War II.

431 **The Air Troop is the parachute division of the SAS.** They are also known as the 'Freefall troop', because when dropped into enemy territory they often delay opening their chutes for as long as possible to avoid detection. They have to jump far behind enemy lines, either to undertake missions themselves or to prepare the way for the regular army.

432 **The motto of the SAS is 'Who Dares Wins'.** The phrase is famous today, but its origins are unknown. Similar phrases appear in the work of ancient Greek playwright Sophocles, and in a letter written by the ancient Roman poet Horace.

◀ The SAS have to be prepared to use tear gas, designed to irritate the eyes and cause difficulty breathing, so may have to wear gas masks.

Respirator

Heckler & Koch MP5 submachine gun

Respirator filter

Bulletproof vest

Leather gloves

433

The SAS carried out a rescue mission on the Iranian embassy in London. On 30 April, 1980, gunmen entered the embassy and took 26 people hostage. Over the next six days five of the hostages were released. Then one was killed by the terrorists and the government ordered the SAS to take action. SAS soldiers swarmed down ropes from the roof and burst through the windows, guns at the ready. The mission lasted 17 minutes. During this time another hostage was killed by one of the terrorists, but all other hostages were freed and all but one of the gunmen were killed.

▲ The SAS made the headlines when they burst into the Iranian embassy in London in 1980 to rescue hostages from gunmen. The man on the left is an escaping hostage, those on the right are SAS.

434

The Boat Troop is the boat section of the SAS. They use small inflatable and rigid boats, and their tasks include dropping and picking up special forces soldiers by water, spying underwater, sinking enemy ships, and fighting terrorism at sea. There is a fierce rivalry between the Boat Troop and the sailors of the SBS, but they often go on missions together.

▶ The badge of the Special Reconnaissance Regiment shows the helmet of an ancient Greek hoplite soldier and the legendary King Arthur's sword, Excalibur.

435

The Special Reconnaissance Regiment is a new and secretive special forces unit. Their main role is to observe and gather information on potentially dangerous people and situations. Their most important task is to keep terrorists under surveillance and they use the latest electronic spying equipment. They are the only special forces unit that admits women.

▼ The Special Boat Service's new superboat can reach 110 kilometres per hour and avoids radar detection with special 'stealth' technology.

436 American special forces units include the Green Berets, Delta Force and SEALs. No outsider knows the full range of units, as some are top-secret. There are even unfounded rumours that there is a special force that relies on telepathy – communication using the power of thought. All US special forces are overseen by the Special Operations Command (SOCOM).

437 The Green Berets specialize in unconventional warfare. This means that they fight more like guerrillas (armed rebel forces) than regular soldiers. Their tactic is to hit targets by surprise in quick raids. The US Army says they work at 'subversion, sabotage, intelligence gathering, escape and evasion'. By this they mean that the role of the Green Berets is to enter enemy territory, create problems, gather information, and get away.

QUICK-FIRE QUIZ

1. How many officers are there in an A-team?
2. What does SOCOM stand for?
3. How many kilometres do Delta Force recruits have to cover in their final training march?

Answers:
1. Two 2. Special Operations Command 3. 64 kilometres

▼ The American Green Berets are trained to cope with the toughest conditions. Here they are training not only to survive in the icy waters of a marsh, but to carry on fighting without tiring.

438 A-teams are key to US special forces. An A-team consists of two officers and ten sergeants. Each team member is chosen and trained to create a broad range of skills across a team, so that every team can operate independently in hostile territory. Different teams specialize in different kinds of mission, from combat diving to mountain warfare.

▶ In the 'Drown Proofing Test', SEAL trainees are dropped into a tank with their hands and feet tied. They have to keep bouncing off the bottom of the tank to surface and catch their breath, until they manage to free themselves and swim to safety.

439 **The US Navy SEALs work mostly on or in water.** Many SEALs are highly trained divers, able to approach tricky targets underwater. In the first Gulf War (1990–1991), a small group of SEALs created a fake attack on the beaches of Kuwait. They succeeded in fooling the Iraqi army into thinking the US attack was coming from the sea.

440 **Delta Force is an elite unit whose task is to combat terrorism, along with the US Navy SEALs.** Delta Force recruits have to endure extremely tough training, similar to that of the British SAS. Training finishes with a gruelling 64-kilometre march across rough terrain, wearing a rucksack that weighs 20 kilograms. Those who complete the march are then subjected to extensive psychological testing.

441 **The Americans insist there are four truths about special forces.** These are: that humans are more important than hardware; that quality is better than quantity; that special operations forces cannot be mass-produced; and that competent special operations forces cannot be created after emergencies occur.

▼ The Search and Rescue team are sent into operations to fly soldiers and airmen to safety. Here they are rehearsing the rescue of a crashed pilot under enemy fire using a CH-53E Super Stallion helicopter.

AROUND THE WORLD

442 **Sayeret Matkal is a unit of the Israeli Defence Force.** In July, 1976, hijackers forced an airliner carrying 246 people to land at Entebbe airport in Uganda. They held the hostages at the airport's old terminal. Sayeret Matkal soldiers flew into the airport in disguised planes, and approached the old terminal in a fleet of cars. The hijackers thought the cars were the escort of Ugandan president, Idi Amin, who supported them, so did not react. The operatives killed the hijackers and flew off with the hostages.

443 **Russia's key special force is called Spetsnaz.** Until 1991 its main role was to spy on and kill enemies of the government. It was also used to fight guerrillas in the mountains of Afghanistan in the 1980s. It is now considered to be one of the world's best counter-terrorist forces.

▶ The Russian Spetsnaz includes some of the world's most accurate and highly trained snipers. Here, a soldier prepares to fire.

444 France's GIGN counter-terrorist force are policemen, not soldiers, but they are famous for their sniping skills. In 1976, a school bus was hijacked in Djibouti, East Africa. The hijackers were allowing food to be sent in for the children, so the GIGN sent sandwiches containing tranquilizers (drugs that send you to sleep). The tranquilized children fell asleep in their seats, giving the GIGN sniper team a clear view to kill the terrorists and rescue the children. Sadly, one little girl was killed too.

A German GSG–9 soldier competes in the World SWAT Challenge to find the worlds best special forces.

▲ Sayeret Matkal insignia

445 Australia's main special force is the Special Air Service Regiment (SASR). Inspired by the SAS, they became known as the 'eyes and ears of the Australian Task Force' (the main Australian army) during the Vietnam war (1965–1975). Now its main task is to fight against terrorism.

446 Germany's GSG–9 were formed after a police attempt to rescue a group of athletes taken hostage at the 1972 Munich Olympics went tragically wrong. One of the GSG–9's most famous missions occurred in 1977, when hijackers forced an airliner to fly to Mogadishu, Somalia. While the hijackers were distracted by a fire in front of the plane, GSG–9 soldiers sneaked onto the wings using rubber ladders. Then they burst into the plane and fired stun grenades to knock everyone out. They killed all but one of the terrorists and rescued all the hostages.

Turkish special forces in operation against Kurdish guerrillas, Turkey.

MAKING THE GRADE

447 **Recruits to the British SAS are put through a gruelling selection process.** Only one applicant out of 12 is successful, even though most are trained soldiers. A potential recruit's first task is to walk 10 kilometres rapidly across country, carrying a rifle and heavy rucksack. And it gets much tougher – applicants are only allowed four hours of sleep before they are sent off on the next task.

448 **If someone makes it through the first week of selection, he is sent on Test Week.** This ends in the dreaded 'Long Drag', in which applicants march for 60 kilometres over Pen-y-Fan, the highest point in the Brecon Beacons, Wales. The Long Drag must be completed in 20 hours, while carrying a 25-kilogram pack (bergen). It's so tough that men have died trying to complete it. The recruiters say, 'We don't try to fail you, we try to kill you.'

449 **To test navigation and map-reading skills, applicants have to find their way to a target through swamps and forest in pitch darkness.** No one is permitted to use a Global Positioning System (GPS) – an electronic navigation gadget – and anyone who goes near a road is instantly failed.

▶ Members of the special forces need to be skilled using weapons but also in hand-to-hand fighting. Here, Korean special forces are trained in martial arts.

450

A special forces soldier has to be an expert fighter. Potential recruits have to complete intensive combat training, where they learn skills such as hand-to-hand combat and fighting with a knife. The standards demanded are very high, and anyone who fails to make the grade is kicked out.

451

The toughest part of the SAS selection process is jungle training in Brunei, Southeast Asia. Applicants are sent into the jungle in groups of four. They have to spend two weeks hacking through thick undergrowth and wading through swamps in soaring temperatures. During jungle training potential recruits may have to contend with dangerous animals and poisonous plants. Many have to be rescued.

452

In the final test, applicants have to live off the land for seven days while evading capture by pursuing soldiers. No one has yet succeeded completely. When caught, applicants are submitted to hours of gruelling interrogation. Finally, they are rescued by their colleagues. This test is called Survive, Evade, Resist, Extract (SERE).

TRAINING FOR ACTION

453 **Fitness is a big part of special forces training.** Recruits train to build strength and go on long marches to increase endurance. Even before selection, applicants must be able to do 40 push-ups in two minutes and run 12.8 kilometres in two hours, while carrying a 21-kilogram pack and a 4-kilogram rifle!

▲ Submachine guns such as the old Heckler & Koch MP5 are key weapons.

► Stun grenades are used to knock enemies out for vital seconds while an attack is made.

454 **A recruit has to master a range of weapons.** These include specialist equipment for use in hostage-rescue missions. Soldiers learn to use items such as stun grenades, tear gas, explosives and shotguns.

455 **The 'Killing House' sounds like the name of a horror film, but it is actually part of British SAS training.** The US Green Berets' version is called the 'House of Horrors'. It is a purpose-built house for use in training special forces soldiers to rescue hostages. The walls inside are moveable, and walls and doors are coated in rubber to absorb gunfire safely. There are fans to take out gun smoke, and a variety of traps can be set to catch operatives if they do not follow correct procedures.

A training raid on a house in complete darkness using night vision equipment.

456 **Special forces soldiers must be able to mount an attack on any target, from a skyscraper to a plane.** Exceptional climbing skills are essential so that soldiers can enter buildings by climbing up a wall or abseiling (speeding down on a rope) from the roof. New recruits practise 'tubular assaults' – training on mock-ups of tube-shaped vehicles in preparation for potential hostage situations on planes, trains and buses.

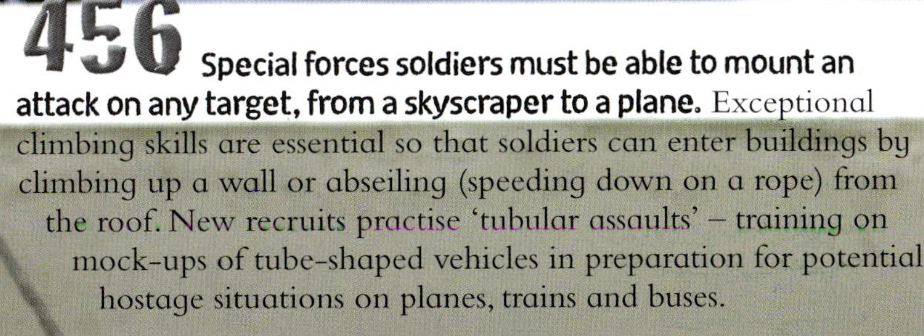

Often, establishing a good relationship with locals is as important as fighting. Here a US soldier hands out crayons in Afghanistan.

◄ A member of Bangkok's special commando unit dives off the top of a building during a training exercise. He holds a tool for breaking windows and his gun at the ready.

457 **Throughout training, special forces soldiers work on their language skills.** Missions may take them to foreign countries, or require international cooperation. Soldiers working abroad may have to give instructions to civilians, or ask them for information, or simply establish good relations with the local population. Any problems with language could be disastrous, so teams often include members fluent in a range of languages.

458 **Four is the best number of men for a small patrol.** Smaller patrols move faster and can hide more easily, but you need at least four people to carry the necessary supplies and equipment. Having four people also means that if one of the group is injured, two people can carry him while the fourth keeps watch.

Each patrol member must cover a certain area with his gun.

459 **To ensure protection from all directions, each soldier covers an angle of visibility with his gun.** The last man ('tailend charlie'), is usually armed with a machine gun to provide covering fire in case of attack from behind. Every 30 minutes, the soldiers lie down to form a circle with each person facing outwards. They observe their surroundings, listening intently for any sound that suggests they are being followed. This is called 'all-round defence'.

▲ A routine four-man foot patrol by Turkish commandos in the mountains on the Turkish border.

460 **A patrol is most likely to be attacked at dawn.** Darkness just before dawn provides cover for enemy soldiers to creep close, and sunrise gives enough visibility to launch an attack. Patrols need to be ready to move just before dawn. Then they 'stand to' for 30 minutes, watching carefully with weapons ready. When the sun is up and all is clear they can move off.

▲ Royal Marines of 45 Commando patrol for enemy soldiers in the mountains of southeastern Afghanistan.

461

Patrol members are trained to act instantly if ambushed. If a patrol is under attack in an area where taking cover isn't an option, soldiers must try to dodge the first bursts of enemy fire and run straight forwards, over the top of the enemy. This kind of quick reaction has saved the lives of many ambushed special forces soldiers.

462

Patrols memorize tactics so they can react instantly. The patrol commander is in charge, but in tricky situations there may not be time to issue orders. Soldiers are trained to know what to do in potential crises without being told. Every unit has its own book of tactics, or 'Standard Operating Procedures', which soldiers have to memorize, as any hesitation or mistake could be fatal.

463

Setting up a perfect ambush (surprise attack) may take weeks. Good locations have plenty of cover, and few escape routes for the target. Patrols may lay mines to cause the target to stop at a certain point, where soldiers are placed in position to prevent the target escaping. A central 'killer' group launches the main attack. Either side of this, support groups provide cover and surround the target. A flanking group prevents attack from the rear.

▼ Learning how to defend yourself effectively against an ambush, called 'ground defence', is a vital part of training for special forces patrols.

464 **Every special forces soldier learns navigation skills.** Today, the SAS exploits global navigation technology such as GPS, which uses satellite signals to pinpoint the user's location. However, some situations may require more old-fashioned skills such as map-reading or navigating by the position of the stars.

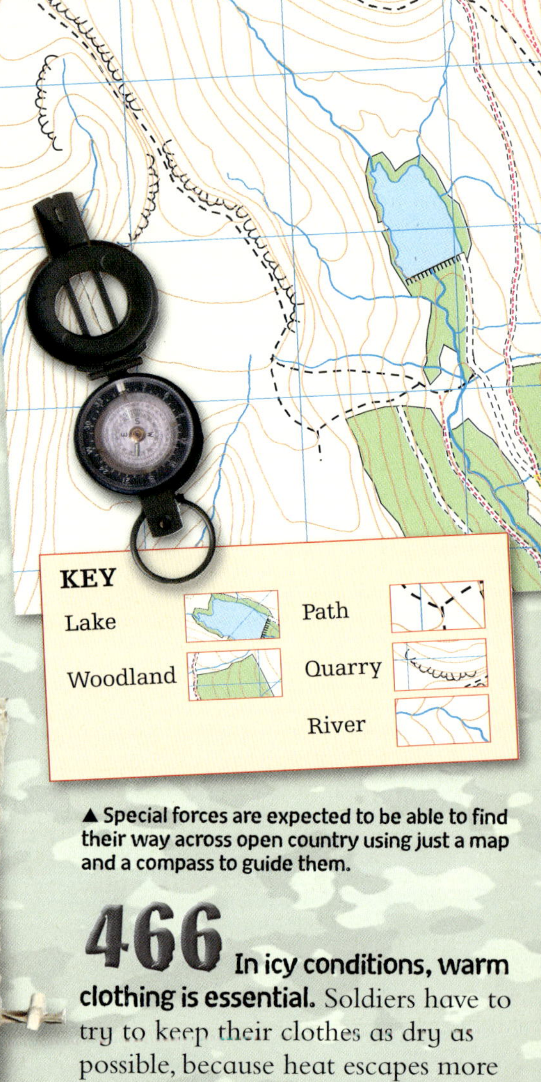

▲ Special forces are expected to be able to find their way across open country using just a map and a compass to guide them.

465 **Special forces soldiers have to be prepared to perform difficult tasks in severe weather conditions.** An operation may require them to cross an icy mountain range during a blizzard, or trek for days through a humid tropical rainforest. To survive such extremes of climate, soldiers have to be physically fit and well prepared. Having the right clothing and equipment may be the difference between life and death.

▶ Fish may be a vital source of fresh food in the wild, so a simple fishing kit can be a life-saver.

466 **In icy conditions, warm clothing is essential.** Soldiers have to try to keep their clothes as dry as possible, because heat escapes more easily from wet clothing. A tent or makeshift shelter is vital for surviving a night in freezing temperatures. Cold winds and sweating from skiing or marching can cause dehydration (insufficient water in the body), so soldiers take fuel to melt snow for water.

467 **If a soldier is alone and far from base, he may have to live off the land.** In this situation, rations (supplies of food and drink) may run out, or have to be made to last for longer than was planned. Soldiers research the plant life in the region of their mission so that they can identify edible wild plants. It is possible to survive for ten days or more without much food, but humans need fresh water daily.

468 **A soldier going on patrol in difficult terrain takes a survival kit.** This typically includes items such as a wire saw for cutting wood, thin wire for making snares to catch animals to eat, basic fishing gear, a flint to light a fire, a candle, a knife, a first aid kit and a compass.

ON THE ATTACK

469 **During wartime, the main task of special forces is sabotage.** This means sneaking into enemy territory to attack key points, such as railway lines. During the first Gulf War, SAS forces were used to sabotage Iraqi radio masts. Under the cover of darkness, armed trucks moved into position as a 'fire support group' (FSG). Meanwhile, an assault team stuck explosives to the masts. The Iraqi guards were alerted, but too late to act. The FSG provided covering fire as the assault team detonated the explosives and retreated.

▼ A view through a telescopic sight.

470 **Soldiers are trained to use explosives, but each patrol also has a demolitions expert.** The type of device used to trigger a bomb depends on the situation. Sometimes a bomb can be set off from a distance using a radio-controlled firing device or an electronic trigger. At other times, soldiers simply light a fuse on the bomb itself before retreating quickly to a safe distance.

▲ Staying hidden is crucial for a sniper. Here snipers are camouflaged pretty effectively as bushes in misty marshland.

471

Snipers are trained to shoot accurately over a long range, from a concealed location. They can hit a target up to one kilometre away, and may have to stalk a target for days before making a shot. To avoid being spotted, snipers wear camouflage, and choose their hiding places carefully.

472

A sniper rifle has a long, heavy barrel so that bullets leave it on the straightest possible path. It also has a telescopic (magnifying) or laser-guided sight for greater accuracy. A sniper rifle is not carried slung on the shoulder, but in a case. This also contains other equipment such as mounts to increase the gun's stability when making a shot.

◀ A sniper rifle is distinguished mainly by its long barrel to ensure accuracy and its telescopic or laser-guided sight to help the sniper find his target.

COUNTERING TERRORISM

473 **Fighting terrorism is the main task of special forces outside of wartime.** This is called 'counter-terrorism'. Terrorists are people who try to make governments or communities do what they want by using violence, such as taking people hostage or blowing up buildings.

▶ Hostages often need to be rescued from inside buildings. It's a dangerous situation and special forces train hard to make an attack with minimum casualties.

474 **The police may be able to prevent acts of terrorism before they happen.** They try to gather information about potential terrorists by keeping them under surveillance (observation). However, terrorists may act before the police can catch them. That's when special forces are called in.

475 **If terrorists take hostages, special forces have to move fast.** If the hostages are being held inside a building, snipers move into position around it to observe the situation and wait for a signal to act. The snipers work in pairs, sending a stream of information back to command. In the British SAS, snipers call terrorists 'X-rays' and hostages 'Yankees'.

476 **When negotiations fail or hostages are in immediate danger, a direct attack may be needed.** Sometimes, 'assaulters' creep in quietly to catch the terrorists by surprise. But if the situation is urgent, they may have to 'go noisy'. That means bursting in quickly, blowing open doors with explosives and throwing stun grenades to overwhelm the terrorists before they have a chance to react.

477 **Piracy is a new threat for special forces to deal with.** There are now pirates in Somalia, on the coast of East Africa, who go out in small boats and attack passing ships. In April 2009, the American captain of the container ship *Maersk Alabama* was kidnapped by pirates. US Navy SEAL special forces raced in and rescued him, killing three of the pirates.

◀ French special forces are seen here in January 2009 capturing 19 Somali pirates before they could make their attack on a ship in the Gulf of Aden.

RAIDING BY WATER

478 **Divers are key in some special forces operations.** Approaching underwater is a good way to pass unseen into enemy territory. Shipping, port facilities and oil rigs are all possible targets for terrorists. Combat divers often have to operate in cold, dark water, and are trained to cope with awkward obstacles and other hazards.

▼ US Navy SEALs burst from the sea in diving suits, guns at the ready for a surprise attack from the water.

▼ A US Navy SEAL, dressed in scuba gear, carries waterproof weapons including a submachine gun, a depth gauge, and an underwater bomb while training.

479 **Combat divers should never have to swim far during a mission.** Swimming is slow and exhausting, so divers are dropped off as close to their target as possible. To avoid detection, they travel by submarine first. Then light, inflatable boats are launched in the darkness to take them closer.

480 **Special forces divers use rebreathers to avoid creating bubbles on the surface of the water.** A rebreather is a device that traps the diver's breath and re-circulates it so that air bubbles don't escape, and give away the diver's position. Equipment of this kind is complex and potentially dangerous, so using it requires a high level of training.

481

Many combat divers use Swimmer Delivery Vehicles (SDVs). These are small submersibles for the transport of combat divers. There are two kinds of SDV – 'wet', where the diver sits astride the SDV exposed to the water, or 'dry', where the diver sits inside. Midget (small) submarines are used for longer missions. Many of these submersibles use stealth technology, which shields them from detection by absorbing or reflecting sonar waves.

▲ A special forces diver gets ready to launch his own Swimmer Delivery Vehicle underwater from a submarine. The SDV is 'wet', and the diver will sit astride it to ride to the target.

482

Small rubber inflatable boats are useful in all kinds of situations. They can be dropped from a helicopter to inflate automatically when they hit the water, or inflated on the decks of submarines. They can be powered by a small outboard motor, or paddled when stealth is needed.

483

A 'Rigid Inflatable Boat' (RIB) has a rigid glass-reinforced plastic (GRP) base to keep its shape. An inflatable tube rim keeps it afloat even if it is swamped by waves. RIBs are much faster and more controllable than small inflatables, but they can't be packed up and dropped so easily from a helicopter or submarine.

▼ Fast and light, rigid inflatable boats (RIBs) are vital for getting small attack groups ashore quickly from ships.

DROPPING FROM THE AIR

484 **The quickest way to get soldiers into position in difficult territory is by parachute.** Paratroopers can be whisked to the furthest corners of the globe and dropped into place in a matter of hours – silently and under cover of darkness if need be. But parachuting can be very dangerous – especially at night and into rugged terrain.

485 **Sometimes paratroopers go HAHO.** This stands for High Altitude High Opening. It means jumping from the plane so high up it can't be seen from the ground, then opening the chute quickly. Modern chutes can be steered by pulling on toggles to glide down slowly over 40 kilometres further on. This way, forces can penetrate deeper into enemy territory than a plane might safely take them. However it is less accurate, and soldiers might get separated from their group on the way down.

▶ In a high-altitude drop a paratrooper needs to wear an oxygen mask to breathe.

To maximize chances of landing together, paratroopers often begin their drop holding hands in free fall before opening their chutes.

486 Sometimes paratroopers go HALO.

This stands for High Altitude Low Opening. It means they will exit the plane at high altitude, then free fall almost to the ground, only opening their chutes at the last minute. Using this method, forces are unlikely to be spotted by an enemy on their way down. Sometimes a group of soldiers may hold hands as they free fall in a 'linked descent' so that they all land in the same drop area.

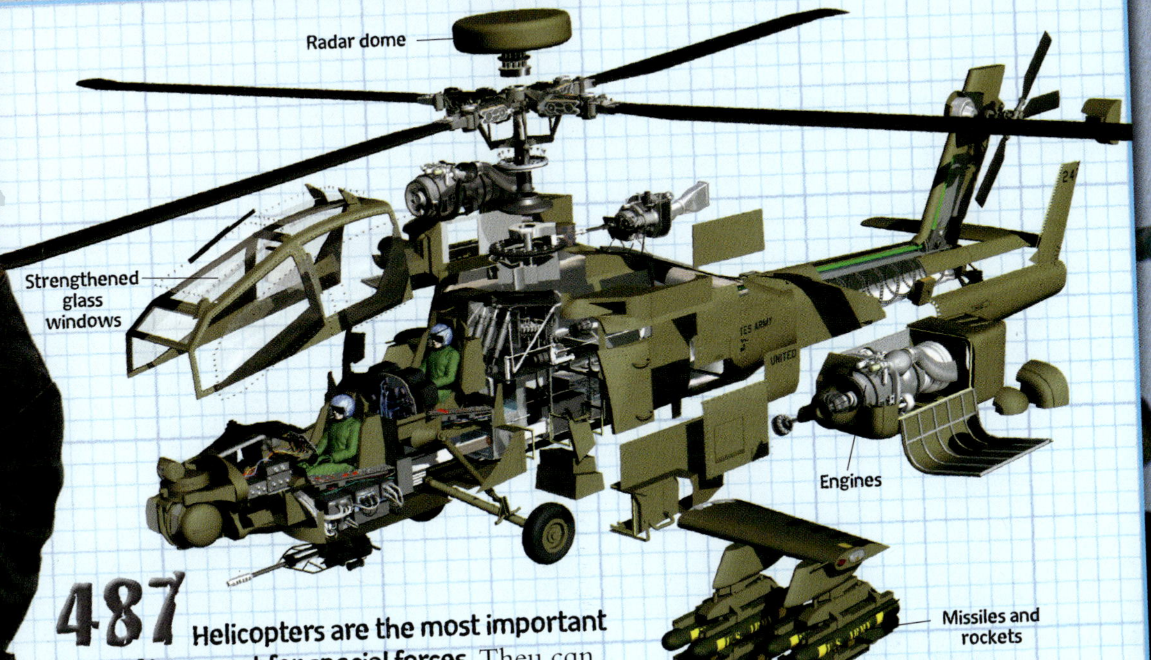

487 Helicopters are the most important form of transport for special forces.

They can whisk men and equipment deep inside enemy territory, then pick them up when the mission is complete. Helicopters can also provide vital covering fire for patrols under attack on the ground, and airlift the wounded to safety.

▲ Attack helicopters such as the AH-64 Apache can provide vital firepower and support for troops on the ground.

STAYING IN TOUCH

488 **A GPS works by electronically comparing the signals from at least four satellites.** With a small hand–held receiver, the user can plot his position to within one metre. In the first Gulf War, US special forces used this technology to guide their tanks into position across the desert, something the Iraqi forces had thought would be impossible.

▲ Laptop computers and telecommunications equipment help special forces locate targets.

489

It is vital that soldiers stay in close personal contact during missions. Every man in a patrol has a digital radio system, allowing him to stay in constant communication with the other members of his team. An earpiece and mouthpiece keeps his hands free. Ordinary soldiers usually only have one radio set per unit, because too much radio traffic can cause confusion, but for special forces, personal radios are vital.

490

A radio signal might give away your position, so modern military radios automatically 'frequency hop' during transmission. This means they continuously change the frequency of the radio waves, making it hard for any eavesdropper to intercept the signal and track the source. Messages are automatically put in code, too, so even if an eavesdropper does pick it up, it's impossible to understand!

◄ The Land Warrior Integrated Fighting System has a helmet display that continually shows the wearer his own location, and that of the enemy.

491

Special forces often guide missiles to their targets. They sneak into enemy territory and pinpoint key objectives, such as missile launch sites. There they set up a piece of equipment called a ground laser target designator. This aims a laser beam at the target and 'paints' it. Computer-guided 'smart' missiles can then see the target and aim for it with pinpoint precision.

► This soldier is using a Guidance Laser Illumination Device (GLID) to paint a target with laser light, which will guide attacking aircraft onto it with pinpoint precision.

INTO THE FUTURE

492 **Batwings are jet-powered personal wings made of carbon-fibre.**
A person wearing them can be dropped from a plane to fly at low-level for hundreds of kilometres. In 2003, Austrian Felix Baumgartner donned batwings and jumped from a plane at an altitude of 10,000 metres over England, landing in France 12 minutes later. However if special forces are using them, they are keeping it secret.

▶ Could special forces soldiers use batwings like these worn by Felix Baumgartner as he glides across the English Channel in 2003?

Sensors in helmet

Video display built into visor

▶ The Future Force Warrior suit may look like something out of science fiction, but soldiers are already trying it out.

493 **The American Future Force warrior system will turn a soldier into superman as soon as he puts on his uniform.** In his helmet, electronic links will tell him his exact location and that of the enemy, as well as what to do at all times. Sensors on his body will relay information back to base to tell medics instantly if he is tired or injured. His liquid body armour will be flexible and easy to move around in — but will turn into rigid protection in a thousandth of a second. An 'exoskeleton' of hydraulic arms attached to his real limbs will give him superhuman strength.

Air filtration system and drinking tube

Body armour

Smart fabric creates a seal that protects the wearer in the event of a chemical attack

494 **Human soldiers may one day be replaced by robot warriors for some tasks.** The iRobot Warrior looks more like a cartoon tank than a soldier. But it can find unexploded bombs, clear mines and explosives, and even go on reconnaissance missions.

495 **Robots can be used instead of soldiers in some tricky situations.** One type of PackBot is used in Iraq to detect bombs. It finds them by making a chemical analysis of the air. Another kind can locate snipers by pinpointing the direction of the sound of the gunshot.

▼ Remotely operated robots are already performing certain tasks such as bomb detection.

FACT AND FICTION

496 **Kit Carson was a real person, but many of the stories told about him are myths.** Carson was a scout in the US cavalry in the early 1800s, who in 1842 helped guide a man called John Fremont to Oregon and California. Fremont wrote accounts of the journey that made Carson sound capable of superhuman feats. He became a national hero.

▶ The cover of a 'Pluck and Luck' book featuring a fictional story about the famous Kit Carson.

▶ A scene from the movie *Black Hawk Down*, which is based on the true story of a mission to rescue the crew of a Black Hawk helicopter shot down in Somalia in 1993.

497 **When Lord Robert Baden-Powell created the Boy Scouts in 1907, he was inspired by stories.** Baden-Powell was the hero of the siege of Mafeking (1899–1900) in the Boer War (1899–1902). He got ideas for the Scouts from seeing the Lovat Scouts in action, and from his friend, writer Rudyard Kipling. 'Kim's game' is an exercise for improving observation by memorizing objects on a tray. Baden-Powell got it from Kipling's story of Kim, the orphan hero of his novel of the same name, set in India.

▶ Founder of the Boy Scouts, Robert Baden-Powell was inspired by Kipling's story of Kim.

SPECIAL FORCES

498 The most famous exploit of special forces in World War II was a daring raid in Norway. The soldiers were dropped in Norway, and they skied across country to destroy a factory making a special kind of liquid that the Germans might have used to make nuclear weapons. The story became the inspiration for a film about a similar raid called *The Heroes of Telemark* (1965).

499 *The Guns of Navarone* (1961) is a film about a fictional World War II raid on a German fortress on a Greek island. In it, the fortress is destroying Allied shipping in the Aegean Sea, but is thought to be impossible to attack. Commandos launch a daring raid to destroy its deadly guns. This story is entirely fictional and based on a novel by the writer Alistair Maclean.

500 *Black Hawk Down* (2001) is a film about an American special forces mission in Mogadishu, Somalia in 1993. It is about a raid that really happened. The aim of the raid was to capture a Somali warlord, Mohamed Farrah Aidid. During the raid, one of the force's Black Hawk helicopters was shot down. American troops invaded to rescue the stranded soldiers. They succeeded, but only after a ferocious battle.

Index

Page numbers in **bold** refer to main entries. Page numbers in *italics* refer to illustrations.

Index

Acknowledgements

The publishers would like to thank the following sources for the use of their photographs:

t = top, b = bottom, l = left, r = right, c = centre, m = main, bg = background, f = far

Page 87 Ninja Museum, Uemo; 133(b) Warner Bros./The Kobal Collection/James, David

The Art Archive 97(t) Rijksmuseum voor Volkenkunde Leiden (Leyden)/Gianni Dagli Orti; 109(b) Bibliothèque des Arts Décoratifs Paris/Gianni Dagli Orti; 113(b); 115(t) and (c) Gunshots; 130–131(b) British Museum; 132(t) Private Collection/Granger Collection

Alamy 10(bc) Jim Cole; 19(tr) North Wind Picture Archives; 34(tr) North Wind Picture Archives; 95 Mary Evans Picture Library; 100 Photos 12; 107 V&A Images; 119(r) Interfoto; 126–127 Photos 12; 130(c) Tibor Bognar; 178(tl) World History Archive; 193(br) A. T. Willett; 195(br) Imagestate Media Partners Limited – Impact Photos

Corbis 33 Gianni Dagli Orti; 34–35 Barry Lewis; 36(br) PoodlesRock; 46 Bettmann; 46–47(tc); 102; 105(t); 106(b) Asian Art & Archaeology, Inc.; 130(t) Sakamoto Photo Research Laboratory; 182(br); 185(bl) Bettmann; 188(cl) Patrick Ward; 189(cl); 191(tr) Hulton-Deutsch Collection; 192(b) JP Laffont/Sygma; 193(t) Lance Iversen/San Francisco Chronicle; 199(m) Reuters; 204(m) Third Eye Images; 206(m) Third Eye Images; 207(br) HO/Reuters; 208(c) Louie Psihoyos, (b) Jim Sugar; 212(m); 213(tl) Ed Quinn, (b) Ed Darack/Science Faction; 215(b) Brian Snyder/Reuters

Dreamstime.com 198(bl) Fotokate; 209(tbg) Irochka

Fotolia.com 19(br) Alfio Ferlito; 184(tl) Samantha Grandy; 188–189(b) Thaut Images

Getty Images 42–43 Bogdan Willewalde; 44–45 Rajesh Jantilal/AFP; 128(t) Hiroshi Higuchi; 181(br); 186(tr) Popperfoto; 190(b); 200(m); 201(tl), (br); 205(tm) MILpictures by Tom Weber; 209(tr) Stocktrek Images; 210(r) Time & Life Pictures; 214–215(tc)

iStockphoto.com 38(tr) Constance McGuire; 42(tl) HultonArchive; 182(l) ChuckSchugPhotography; 183(bfr) DoctorQ; 184–185(t) Rockfinder; 185(br) Richcano; 186–187(bc) Mettus; 187(tl) Linda Steward; 188(bl) Duncan1890; 190–191(bc) SpxChrome; 192–193(tc) Liliboas; 196(tl) Jane; 198(bg) AndreasG; 202(tl) Krakozawr, (bl) Ollikainen; 204(cr) Makhnach/Macsek; 208(t) 2ndLookGraphics; 212–213(bg) Dinn; 212(tr) Axstokes; 214–215(bg) Foundation7

Moviestore Collection Ltd 8–9 Warner Bros. Pictures; 17(r) Warner Bros. Pictures; 29(b) Twentieth Century-Fox Film Corporation; 48(l) New Line Cinema; 48–49 Lucasfilm; 49(br) Twentieth Century-Fox Film Corporation; 216–217(m) Revolution Studios

photolibrary.com 103(c); 105(b) JTB Photo; 120(c) Corbis

Rex Features 183(br); 191(b) Bournemouth News; 194–195(b) Dmitry Beliakov; 195(tl) Action Press; 196–197(m) Sipa Press; 205(tl); 209(b) Greg E. Mathieson; 210(l) Sipa Press

TopFoto 18–19 Warner Bros. Pictures; 37 TopFoto/HIP; 40(tr) The British Library/HIP; 45(tl) The Granger Collection; 131(t) Print Collector/HIP; 176–177 Â©RIA Novosti; 184(tr); 184–185(bc) Â©2006 Alinari; 216(tr) The Granger Collection/New York

All other photographs are from: Corel, digitalSTOCK, digitalvision, Fotolia.com, ImageState, iStockphoto.com, John Foxx, PhotoAlto, PhotoDisc, PhotoEssentials, PhotoPro, PhotoSphere, Stockbyte

Every effort has been made to acknowledge the source and copyright holder of each picture. Miles Kelly Publishing apologises for any unintentional errors or omissions.

All artworks from the Miles Kelly Artwork Bank